ILLEGIT

A MEMOIR OF FAMILY INTRIGUE, WEALTH, AND CRUEL INDIFFERENCE

GEORGE A. DEMOULAS

Copyright © 2024 George A. DeMoulas.

All rights reserved. No part of this book may be reproduced, stored, or transmitted by any means—whether auditory, graphic, mechanical, or electronic—without written permission of both publisher and author, except in the case of brief excerpts used in critical articles and reviews. Unauthorized reproduction of any part of this work is illegal and is punishable by law.

ISBN: 979-8-89031-888-6 (sc)
ISBN: 979-8-89031-889-3 (hc)
ISBN: 979-8-89031-890-9 (e)

Library of Congress Control Number: 2014914278

Because of the dynamic nature of the Internet, any web addresses or links contained in this book may have changed since publication and may no longer be valid. The views expressed in this work are solely those of the author and do not necessarily reflect the views of the publisher, and the publisher hereby disclaims any responsibility for them.

One Galleria Blvd., Suite 1900, Metairie, LA 70001
(504) 702-6708

AUTHOR'S NOTE

People write memoirs for many reasons but mostly because they want to share their stories. That's the case with me. I am not afraid to tell what happened to me, my siblings, and my mother as a result of being subjected to cruel indifference and poverty simply because the wealthy man who was my father decided he didn't want to take responsibility for his mistress and the five children he had with her. I'm not afraid to tell you that the anger and confusion I felt because of my upbringing in a run-down housing project in Lowell, Massachusetts, led me to a life of drug and alcohol addiction that nearly killed me. What saved me was my deep commitment to seek justice against all odds.

As I sit down to write this book, I am proud to say that I have been clean and sober since 1988. I have prevailed against my father and his family, at least to the extent currently possible under the law. I have claimed my rightful name.

PROLOGUE

The call came in while I was on vacation in Palm Beach, seeking a short respite in sunny Florida from the ongoing battle I'd been waging with a side of my family that wished I didn't exist. I was struggling in court to get some sort of justice, some sort of acknowledgement that I truly was a member of the DeMoulas clan, a cadre of superrich who'd made their fortune in the food business. I held the phone tighter and tighter as I listened to my brother's news. My long-estranged father, John DeMoulas, had died at the age of eighty-four. It was March 8, 2000.

I can describe the journey up to that point only as long, painful, and full of rage on my part. Why, I wondered, did I have to fight in court to amend my birth certificate to reflect my true last name? Why couldn't my family simply admit that I was of their blood, that my father had carried on an affair with my mother for many years and had produced a brood of kids along the way? I wanted no money. I wanted no part of their lives. I just wanted my rightful name, and I was fighting to get it.

Just hours after John's death, before his body could be cremated, under a court order my attorney obtained, the right and left sides of John's mouth were swabbed for DNA. The samples were sealed in a plastic bag and sent via overnight mail to the Laboratory Corporation of America test facilities in Burlington, North Carolina. That conclusive act was to become the defining and final chapter in an incredible saga of lies and deception involving one of the wealthiest families in New England.

When the DNA results came back, it was clear to all involved that John was my biological father. Despite nearly overwhelming obstacles, I, the bastard son, had prevailed.

ONE

All stories start at the beginning. It is like that for families as well. Families don't just appear in a flash. There is a continuum that reaches back through time to long before the newest members of the family are born. So it is with my story. It all began in Greece with my paternal grandfather, Athanasias Demoulas. He was born in 1883 in a small village in the shadows of the Meteora and the Pindus Mountains, which are located in the central part of the country. The region is renowned for its ancient monasteries and has been described as "the perfect place for Zeus to store his thunderbolts."

When he was twenty-three, Athanasias immigrated to America, landing on Ellis Island in the shadows of the Statue of Liberty on St. Patrick's Day in 1906. At the time of my grandfather's passage to America, his homeland and its neighbors were embroiled in the endemic rivalry that still persists in the Balkans. Serbs, Slavs, Bosnians, Albanians, and Bulgarians all were involved in the ongoing battles, and Greek guerrillas were on a rampage in the mountains of Macedonia. Although I do not know for certain what prompted my grandfather to leave Meteora, his family, and his childhood sweetheart, who was to become my grandmother, it seems evident the sociopolitical turmoil and the harsh economic conditions in his homeland played a role in his decision.

Soon after arriving in New York, Athanasias made his way to Lowell, Massachusetts, following in the footsteps of thousands of immigrants, many Greeks among them. Lowell was then known as Spindle City because of the dozens of textile mills that extended for miles along the edge of the Merrimac River. The Greek, French, Irish, and French-Canadian immigrants who toiled in those mills congregated in a section of Lowell called the Acre, which stretched from Lowell City Hall along Market Street toward the river.

My grandfather soon found work in a tannery as a shoemaker and, within three years, had saved enough money to send for the girl he had left behind in Meteora. Tall and thin and eleven years his junior, my grandmother was Efrosine Souleiman. Shortly after her arrival in Lowell, she and Athanasias were married. At some point along the path to assimilation, my grandfather began to refer to himself as Athas, a name far easier for people to pronounce than Athanasias. Later still, he went by Arthur, a name eventually passed on to two of his grandsons. My mother also gave it to me as my middle name. As I look back on this part of my family history, information I learned only after years of searching public records and gleaning what I could from my mother, I find myself feeling sad sometimes. The story of my grandfather is rich in the stuff of the American dream. I am part of that story, yet it is as if my siblings and I never existed. In that sense, we lived in a world devoid of the grounding most of us depend on for the rudiments of our self-identities. It's a strange and sad place to be when you're adrift and ignored.

My grandfather worked hard in the tannery for years, but his health began to suffer. The working conditions in the factory were awful, and his doctor advised Arthur to leave his job. In 1917, at the age of thirty-four and eleven years after he had arrived in Lowell, my grandfather opened Demoulas Market on Dummer Street in the Acre and began selling meat, produce, and sundries to his fellow émigrés from Greece and other parts of the world. Above the awning on the front of the shop hung a sign advertising "Lamb, Sausages & Pork." Arthur and Efrosine did their own slaughtering, and several times each week, my grandfather drove his battered old Ford truck to the railroad yards to pick up live sheep and pigs. They kept chickens in wooden cages on the sidewalk outside the shop. After selecting a chicken, customers brought it inside to be weighed and then carried it off, alive and squawking, wrapped up in sheets of newspaper. In time, my grandmother became renowned for her roasted pork sandwiches, a specialty favored by the workers who passed by the shop on their way to the mills.

In keeping with the custom among many merchants in immigrant cities, Arthur allowed his customers to buy on credit, and he delivered their purchases free of charge. It was a different time, a different world. I don't want to romanticize those times too much, but it always strikes me that life must have been somehow more wholesome. Of course, life was just as hard then as it is now. With America's entry into the War to End All Wars, Lowell's economy surged, and in 1918, Arthur and Efrosine were able to realize their dream of owning property. They bought a farm in the nearby town of Dracut, where they raised cows, pigs, goats, chickens, and ducks.

Over the next fifteen years or so, the Demoulas Market continued to flourish. My grandparents had several children. My father, John, was born in 1915. His brother George followed in 1919, and Telemachus came along in 1920 and always went by the name of Mike. My grandmother tragically lost three other children due to illness, which was not uncommon back then.

Throughout the 1920s, the store did well. By all accounts, the family was happy. The three boys played in the neighborhood with friends, went to school, and messed about, as all kids do. They also worked in the store, which turned a small profit even in the early part of the Great Depression. However, by 1938, things had taken a turn for the worse. So many of my grandparents' customers were in debt to them that they were unable to pay their own bills. The bank threatened to take their farm unless they paid the $100 they owed on their mortgage. They somehow averted the crisis, but like many of their generation, my grandparents grew even more resistant to moving too fast or wanting too much.

As soon as they graduated from high school, my uncles George and Mike went to work full-time in my grandparents' store. My grandparents allowed John to follow another more-independent path, something he would do throughout his life. In the Greek culture, for centuries, the oldest male child had enjoyed special patriarchal status. As the firstborn, my father was, without question, the favored son, and for his entire life, he was to have an inherited and inherent authority over his two younger brothers and his younger sister.

The miseries of the Great Depression faded into the past with the United States' entrance into World War II. Lowell, as it had been two and a half decades earlier, was the beneficiary of the economic boom brought about by the demands for its contributions to the necessities of battle.

After Pearl Harbor, Uncle George enlisted in the army, and when the war ended, he returned to work in the store alongside his parents and brother Mike. (For reasons unclear to me, neither my father nor Uncle Mike served in the war.)

The late 1940s gave rise to an increasing number of supermarket chains, and because of their superior buying power, these chains were ringing the death knell of the small independents. The bell did not toll for my grandparents, however; the Demoulas Market on Dummer Street in Lowell continued to prosper. Arthur and Efrosine prospered; they continued working long, hard hours at the market and on the farm where they were raising their children. In 1950, they built a new store on the site of the original Demoulas Market and, four years later, sold the business to George and Mike for $15,000. Mike assumed the title of president, and George became treasurer. When Mike and George decided to expand the market two years later, they did so against the advice of several local businessmen, including my grandfather, prompting him to complain to a friend, "What are they doing? Have they lost their minds?"

While Mike and George were focusing on building the business, my father, John, married and opened a restaurant and bar named Marion's Café, after his wife. Sometime thereafter, he purchased a second business, the Golden Nugget Lounge, and then real estate in New Hampshire and Florida. In addition to his obvious skills as a businessman, my father was also handsome, incredibly charming, and remarkably coldhearted—attributes that would ultimately seal my mother's fate and propel her and her illegitimate children into a life of misery.

And it all started because of political and social unrest in Greece at the turn of the last century. My grandparents had established a good business. They'd run it with clear heads and the sweat of hard work, and then they'd passed it down to two of their sons, establishing a legacy they were proud of. They'd also unwittingly planted the seeds that would grow into the oak of a mighty financial empire, though if you'd told them that when they retired, they'd have just laughed.

TWO

My mother, Dorothy Bedard, was Irish. She was born in Lowell in 1933, the youngest of ten children. She had beautiful platinum-blonde hair and sparkling green eyes. When I look at pictures taken of her as a young woman, she reminds me of Grace Kelly—beautiful and fragile. It is no surprise that my father was taken with her upon their first meeting. The two of them became caught up in the magic of romance. She was the beautiful blonde, and he was the handsome gentleman of means. He was somewhat short and stocky but debonair, and his thick mustache gave him something of the look of Clark Gable. I think he represented a sort of untouchable to my mother, the kind of man she could only dream of. When he invited her to his bed, she went willingly, and she did not want to leave the fantasy even when the good dream of what she could never have went straight to hell.

I can't blame my mother for what she did, for how she ignored what most sensible people would have finally come to realize. As I said, the story starts with the family continuum. It starts with a circumstance beyond the control of the person, the individual—the group we call family. The conditions my mother grew up with, which included abject poverty and, more significantly, a family incapable of loving, scarred her for life. What would her life have been like if she had been born into a family that cared? What would my life have been like? Sadly, late at night, when I can't sleep, I look up at the ceiling in the dark of my bedroom, and I can imagine the alternate universe where life might have been different, a little less tortured and full of rage. But the imagined is not the reality any of us face. We face what we have, whether we like it or not.

When she was in sixth grade, my mother was diagnosed with a heart murmur and left school. Thereafter, she stayed home— more often than not, all alone in a cold, dark tenement. When she was fifteen, she forged work papers and took a job as a factory girl at Roby Shoes in Lowell. Every dime she earned went toward supporting her family. Four years later, in the spring of 1952, Sophie Irons, an older woman who had befriended my mother, invited her for a drink after work at Marion's Café. There, on that fateful day, Sophie introduced my mother to the proprietor, my father, John Demoulas.

At the time they met, my father was in his late thirties. Although my mother was aware he was married, she fell hopelessly in love with him. From that moment, she became entangled in a life that was sometimes the stuff of dreams and other times overwhelming and frightening. Perhaps, at age nineteen, she saw in John Demoulas the answer to her prayers—the hope that somehow he might be the answer to her leaving behind the life of misery she saw stretching endlessly ahead. We all face times of desperation and despair. We all cling to the hope that our lives might one day improve. When the hand of possibility reaches out, we take it even though we know in our hearts that we're doing wrong. I think Dorothy knew all along that she was standing on the edge of an emotional cliff when she met and fell in love with John, but she wanted so badly to get into a life with hope that she willingly stepped right off into thin air. She fell, and she held on to John's hand until he let her go.

In retrospect, from my perspective as a grown man, I can say with clarity that my father saw in her an opportunity to take advantage of a naive, desperate, and beautiful young woman. John was a coldhearted son of a bitch. He knew what he wanted when he saw it, and he took it. I know this from my personal experiences with him and his brothers as I grew up in the shadow of a burgeoning family empire. I know this because my mother and I used to talk long into the night about the forces that shaped both of our lives. I know this because I lived it, and I don't think I am alone in what I experienced. Few families are without blemish. Life simply isn't like that. You never know what goes on behind closed doors, even if those doors close the world off from the fortress of a palatial mansion.

Not long after John and Dorothy met, my father gave my mother a job tending bar at the café—a profession she engaged in on and off for the rest of her working days. He then installed her in a rented apartment at 10 Davis Street in Lowell, an address decidedly on the wrong side of the tracks. Confident in his position as the eldest son and a popular and respected figure in his social circles, my father apparently was unconcerned about appearances, at least not among his friends and business associates. I have no way of knowing whether his wife or my grandparents were aware of the relationship at that point in time. I suppose it doesn't matter. I do wonder, though. John was unafraid of most things. I doubt he would have cared if his parents or his brothers had known he was cheating on his wife. My older sister Melveen was in born in Lowell at Shaw Hospital on

June 22, 1954, less than two years after my mother and father met. My mother was twenty-one years old.

Dr. Adam Shaw founded the hospital in the early twentieth century as a private maternity hospital, a place where women who found themselves in compromised positions were accepted without questions being asked. A Dr. Vergaropoulos delivered an unnamed baby girl at 12:30 a.m. My mother's name is the only name listed on the birth certificate. According to that document, the baby's father was unknown. My father and his attorney, James Curtis, arranged for the baby girl's placement, and filed in the hospital records along with the birth certificate was an affidavit that gave the right to "the people listed on the legal papers to take our baby daughter."

The affidavit was signed by Dorothy Bedard and John Demoulas and witnessed by G. H. McAllister and Mrs. John Hickey. It is dated June 26, 1954, four days after Melveen was born. Many years later, that piece of paper was to be a critical piece of evidence in a lengthy legal battle played out in a Cambridge, Massachusetts, courtroom. My mother says that when they took her baby away, it was the hardest thing she ever experienced in her life. And for a day or so after the birth, my mother was led to believe that she and John would leave Lowell for California to start a new life together.

According to my mother, it was my father's brother, my uncle Mike, who advanced this plan in order to protect the family name. The Demoulases, of course, were highly respected members of the greater Lowell community. The market was booming, and George and Mike had recently opened a new store. They had great plans for even more expansion. They did not want scandal or responsibility for their older brother's misdeeds. John played both ends, placating his family and my mother. It was a clear case of him wanting to have his cake and eat it, too. When Uncle Mike visited her in the hospital, it soon became clear to my mother that my father had no intention of leaving Lowell.

"I'm warning you, Dorothy," he told her. "Stay away from John."

My mother recalls yelling at him, "Listen, it's John who can't stay away from me!"

There's ample evidence of the truth of her answer. Melveen was only the first of five bastard children to be born to my mother and father. More than forty years would pass before my mother was to see Melveen again.

In 1955, a year after my sister Melveen was born, my uncles Mike and George expanded the superette on Dummer Street once again. This time, the store tripled in size. It comprised 33,600 square feet of display space and two checkout counters. An impressive new sign—DeMoulas Super Market—hung across the facade. For some unknown reason, perhaps to add a bit of distinction, they changed the *m* in *Demoulas* to a capital *M*. The brothers were on their way to fulfilling a promise they had made to each other to build a supermarket empire. Several years later, Mike and George built a second DeMoulas Market on Bridge Street, just a few blocks away from the Dummer Street location. My grandfather Arthur, looking frail and weary, cut the ribbon during the grand-opening ceremony. He died six months later at age seventy-five.

Over time, my uncles Mike and George continued to expand the DeMoulas chain, often opening two or three stores in a single year. Although my father continued to distance himself from any direct involvement in the family business, the family always gave him the opportunity to open a liquor store next door to the new stores, an opportunity he always took advantage of. Frankly, John got the best deal out of the three brothers. George and Mike did the work, and John cashed the checks from the liquor stores, which prospered because they were right next to thriving grocery stores. As the oldest brother, he was seen as the leader of the family, even though he did not deserve such a distinction.

When Arthur died, my grandfather still owned a percentage of the business, and Mike and George inherited it all. He left my father no part of it. From what I can determine, there had been a falling out between my grandfather and my father at some point, although I do not know the nature of the dispute. I can guess, however, that my grandfather did not approve of the way my father had chosen to live his life. Perhaps Arthur was aware of my father's philandering; he certainly was aware of the increasingly important role liquor played in both my father's business and personal life. My grandmother, however, adored her firstborn son and assured him that he would be cared for after her death. She died in 1964.

Over the ensuing years, my father and his wife, Marion, had four children: Jack, Arthur, Pamela, and Kathleen—several remarkably close in age to my siblings. John was leading a double life. He knew it, and Dorothy knew it. She let him dole out meager funds for a crappy apartment and a little food, and she always dreamed and hoped that one day he would come to love her as much as she loved him. In many ways, she was weak. She lacked the strength to stand her ground against a man who was clearly using her— with her permission, I might add. She enabled John, and he took full advantage of his situation. She wanted love, just as we all do. She harbored intense guilt for giving Melveen up. Her childhood haunted her. In a sense, she never really had a chance in life. While John raised his other family in the lap of luxury, he and my mother carried on with their affair. In addition to my sister Melveen, the relationship resulted in my older brothers, John and Michael; my older sister Dorothy; my younger sister, Patricia; and me. Why my father allowed my mother to give his first name and those of his two brothers to my brothers and me will forever remain a mystery.

Some years before I was born, my father gave my mother a diamond ring, which she wore on her left hand. He obviously never meant that gesture as any kind of a commitment, but for a time, my mother held out hope that the ring meant that one day she and my father would be together. To her, I think the ring somehow legitimized their relationship. My mother always wondered where my father got that diamond ring. I think she might have suspected it had at one time belonged to his wife, whom he'd perhaps given a bigger ring for putting up with his philandering.

One day, when I was about eight, the diamond fell out of its setting while my mother was doing laundry. She spent hours looking for it and then sobbed into the night, knowing it would never be replaced. She took off the ring and put it inside a small cardboard box on her bureau. She still has that box with the empty ring inside, a reminder of a wedding she never had and a symbol of her happiest and her loneliest memories, all wrapped up in one man.

As time progressed and the Bedard family grew, the DeMoulases made no further attempts to convince either my mother or my father to give up my siblings or me for adoption. Perhaps as my father and his brothers became increasingly wealthy and prominent, they developed a sense that they were no longer subject to any negative impact this ongoing relationship with my mother might have on their reputations. If, indeed, there is any truth to that suspicion, the family was to be proven remarkably wrong. Two of my siblings were also born at Shaw Hospital, and two others were born at St. Joseph's, also in Lowell.

My mother believed that by delivering her babies at two different hospitals, she might somehow escape detection by the state authorities. She was understandably concerned that were they to learn she was giving birth to so many children out of wedlock, those authorities might initiate legal action to remove them from her care. She might have been right, but no one ever came knocking on our door. I seriously doubt that the child-protection-services system ever knew or, if they did, cared one iota about any of us. I was also born at Shaw Hospital, on October 10, 1961. The name on my birth certificate read "George Arthur Bedard."

THREE

I have always wondered why my mother put up with John in those early years of their strange relationship. He clearly used her for sex, as if she were a plaything put on the earth merely to satisfy his lust. He valued her only because she made him feel good on a physical and emotional level. Yet Dorothy kept the relationship intact even when the most obvious thing to do would have been to run screaming from the room. Perhaps, in her defense, the status quo was better than the unknown. After all, things were much different in the late 1950s and early 1960s. Nice girls didn't do what my mother was doing—carrying on with a married man and having not just one but five kids with him. Later, my mother began to fight for us, dragging John to court in an unsuccessful battle to get child support. But in those early years, she was docile.

My older siblings John, Mike, and Dottie remember family trips to the beach and, once, a trip to New York City, where they wrote their initials on the walls of the viewing area on top of the Empire State Building. I can picture them driving to the big city in John's Cadillac, eating ice-cream cones, and gawking at the sights and sounds of Manhattan. Looking back on it now, I find myself wanting to believe that in the early days of their relationship, my father loved my mother in his own way and that they lived a kind of shadow marriage. Obviously, one or the other or both were willing to accept the inevitable results of their lovemaking.

Those times when we were together as a sort of hidden family were infrequent. We almost never saw John. We called him "the Greek" behind his back, and it was not an affectionate term. On the rare occasions we were with him, I don't think we called him anything at all other than perhaps "sir." As a small child, I rarely saw my father, and when I did, it was always a painful experience. As I've said, my three older siblings spent more time with him when they were young than I did, but he remained an elusive figure for all of us.

A few times, my father picked us all up and took us to the Methuen Mall to buy clothes. I have no idea what prompted those outings, but I do know they were always rushed. "Hurry up! Hurry up," he'd keep telling us. I can only guess he was afraid someone he knew might see him with my mother and us.

During those trips, he rarely spoke. I often wonder what he thought driving his big car filled with his bastard children— children who were rough around the edges and needy. As much as we all wanted him to pay at least minimal attention to us, we just sat quietly in the back of his Cadillac, afraid to say much and daring to imagine this family trip to the mall as something like what other, normal families did together.

When my sister Patricia, the last of the bastard Bedard children, was born, she spent the first six months of her life with an aunt, because by this time, my mother was barely able to care for the rest of us. My mother told me that when Patricia was born, she at last began to realize there was to be no happy ending to her relationship to John DeMoulas. While my father and his wife, Marion, brought up our half brothers and sisters in the Greek Eastern Orthodox religion, my mother raised my siblings and me as Catholics, at least in our younger years. Whatever religious groundings we had as children, however, had little, if any, positive impact on our adult lives.

For several years after they were born, my siblings John, Mike, and Dottie lived with my mother in the same furnished apartment on Davis Street in Lowell where my father had installed my mother years before, after they'd first met. My first home, and what was to be the Bedard family home throughout the 1960s and early 1970s, was an apartment in a dark and depressing Lowell housing project named for Bishop Thomas Francis Markham, who had died in 1952. Although I know nothing about him, I suspect Bishop Markham might have preferred his good name not be associated with the miserable conditions we and the other residents of the project were forced to endure. Crime of all descriptions was our daily bread. To this day, I can hear the screams of young girls being assaulted in the dark and feel the penetrating cold of the dank hallways of those brutal buildings. There was no such thing as civil rights for any of us, black, white, or brown.

We lived on the third floor in an apartment that faced the back of the building. When it was working, we took an elevator to the second floor and then walked quickly up one flight to the relative safety of our apartment, flaking black paint peeling off the railings in our hands as we went. The apartment consisted of a small living room, a kitchen, and, down a narrow, dimly lit corridor, three small bedrooms. Seven of us shared the single bathroom. Some sort of dark green rubber covered the floors throughout the apartment, and much like a metaphor for the lives we lived, those floors were both harsh and unforgiving. The kitchen was sparse. Sometimes, in the morning, we'd make toast by dangling slices of bread from a metal clothes hanger over the single working gas burner on the stove—at least that was what we did when we had bread. It was always either too hot or too cold inside the apartment.

What little furniture we had consisted of the white plastic fold-up variety—furniture originally designed for gracious outdoor living. We had no art on the walls, no books, and no shelves or coffee table to put them on. In short, there was virtually nothing in that apartment to soften the harsh realities of the lives we were living. We could have packed up everything we owned and left that apartment behind forever in less than an hour. Unfortunately, for nearly two decades, the Bedard family was never afforded that opportunity.

Unless you've ever been really hungry for days and weeks on end, it isn't possible to comprehend the desolation and panic we felt day in and day out. Ironically, there was a DeMoulas Supermarket less than a mile away from our apartment, but as far as we were concerned, that elusive lifeline might just as well have been a fortress protected by a moat and armed warriors. My family and I lived at the edges of survival. We were where and were what no one ever wants to be.

Even after it became increasingly clear to my mother that John would never marry her, she still clung to the hope in spite of knowing better. It was obvious that more often than not, Dorothy's feelings for John DeMoulas and fantasies of having a future together with him consumed her. At times, she was also drinking heavily. I'd come home from elementary school only to find her sitting alone on her bed at the window, watching and waiting to see if his big black Cadillac would pull up to the curb. Sitting and looking out that window became a kind of ritual. She was willing to do anything for an hour or less with him. Especially in the last years of their relationship, it's highly unlikely he ever told her when or if he was coming, so she waited hopefully every afternoon until darkness enveloped the littered streets below.

One day, when I was ten or eleven, my father pulled up in front of the apartment and honked the horn. For some reason, my mother sent me down to see him. He had brought us our first television set, a cast-off from his vacation house in New Hampshire. It was an old black-and-white set that was barely working. My mother watched that TV every day until it finally died and, for years, kept the remains in a closet.

Some of my earliest memories in life still haunt me now: the horrible apartment, my mother's pathetic love for a man with a heart of stone, the feeling of inferiority and despair we all had as we struggled to live on welfare checks totaling about $300 per month. Every now and then, my father would drop off some money. He also sometimes brought around baskets of food, especially on Thanksgiving and Christmas, but for the most part, we went hungry. For the most part, we huddled in the apartment in the cold, the radiators barely warm in winter, or we roasted at the height of summer. My siblings share similarly disturbing memories, of course, and none of us like to talk about those days.

However, my siblings did tell me about the first of many battles my mother fought against John in court. I was only two years old at the time, so I can't remember what finally got Dorothy to confront John. I suspect it was our abject poverty. Our situation was all the more painful because we knew that John and his family were becoming wealthier every day. They drove fine cars and lived in nice houses. They wanted for nothing while we rotted in the slums.

So on February 13, 1963, against considerable odds, my mother succeeded in bringing my father to court in an effort to seek child support. She and my father remained intimate, but the long affair was beginning to show signs of fading, and according to my older siblings, John and Dorothy began to fight more frequently. The Greek sometimes hit my mother. She always seemed to want him around, even as the relationship became more strained, but we preferred for him to stay away when he got mean, which was often. In any event, whatever affection he continued to have for her did not change the fact that he obviously felt no financial responsibility for her or for us. The pattern of neglect that had marked my father's relationship with my mother from the outset was to prevail to the end.

When asked in court how he pleaded to the charge he had failed to support his minor children, my father said, "Not guilty." After considering the evidence, the judge disagreed and ordered him to begin paying my mother thirty-five dollars a week, but my father simply chose to ignore the court order. My mother was defeated and heartbroken.

As the DeMoulas empire grew to encompass more and more communities throughout Massachusetts and New Hampshire, more and more people became aware of John DeMoulas's relationship with my mother. It's inconceivable that my father's wife wasn't aware of the situation. The Bedard children were hardly the best-kept secret in town. However, if Marion ever gave my father any ultimatums, we never knew about them. My father was drinking heavily at the time, and my uncle Mike, who clearly was in charge of the business that carried the DeMoulas family name, did what he could to control the flow of information about my father.

Try as she might, Dorothy never could get John to pay the child support that the court had ordered. The family was well connected in the town. They knew important people, and they were able to stay above the law.

In total frustration, Dorothy took John to court again. In a second trial, on October 27, 1965, the judge inexplicably reduced the original court order to thirty dollars a week. Despite the fact that my father had ignored the original court order, the judge did not impose any penalties, financial or otherwise, on him. Once again, my father simply ignored the court order.

Three years later, on October 26, 1968, the original case was dismissed. Rather than running the risk of incurring perhaps thousands of dollars in cost pursuing my father, the Lowell court apparently decided to let the Commonwealth of Massachusetts assume responsibility for providing for our basic needs.

FOUR

As the DeMoulas fortunes continued to grow, the family established a foundation, the purpose of which was to provide financial and other support for needy children in Lowell. To those who understood the true motive, it was an incredibly transparent attempt by the DeMoulas family members, especially Uncle Mike and Uncle George, to ingratiate themselves with the community and embellish the DeMoulas name. Frankly, it was a smart move from a public-relations perspective—nobody can ever say my uncles were stupid. They were savvy businessmen, and they were ruthless in their pursuit of wealth and power. News of their generous act came at a particularly low point in our lives, rubbing salt in our wounds in a way that still strikes me as horrendously cruel.

One day, I came home from school without eating lunch, because Dorothy had had no money to give me to spend at the cafeteria. My mother looked terrible as she sat at the kitchen table. She had me sit down next to her as she read a story to me in the local paper, the *Lowell Sun*. After she finished reading, she said, "George, the DeMoulas family is donating one million dollars to the Lowell Boys and Girls Club. One million dollars—and we have nothing to eat tonight. They're giving away a million dollars, and they refuse to take care of us."

The biting pain of that moment lingers in my mind all these years later. I shake my head and still find it almost impossible to fathom how my father could let us rot in poverty while the family made the pretense of being generous to the needy. The hypocrisy is indescribable. I've spent many sleepless nights wondering about the nature of the DeMoulas family, and I have concluded that they were as uncaring as the worst of souls. The sad and obvious irony for our family was that while reports trumpeted the family's largess in the local and Boston press, my father was allowing the state welfare system to pay for feeding and sheltering his children. We might have been bastard children, but we were his children.

I think when she first read that story, my mother came to a real awareness of what she had done to herself and to us, of the terrible mistakes she had made. But my mother had no idea how to deal with the situation we faced. I think at that moment, she finally realized she had failed her family. She realized that John DeMoulas was never going to support her or the children they had brought into this cruel existence. He had a life, and she would never be a part of it—and neither would we.

It was as if all those years of dreaming of a life with this man suddenly, once and for all, vanished forever. She bent over, put her head on the table, and sobbed; her will and her heart were broken beyond repair. I'll never forget that day. I was starving, and I had hunger pains in my stomach. I just sat in my chair, looking at my mother and the tears flowing from her eyes. Then she ran from the room.

I read the article again to myself, trying to put together the strange pieces of the reality that other children—many even less desperate than we were—were going to be beneficiaries of the DeMoulases' great wealth. Looking back on that day, I understand what motivated them to do what they did, but to me, it was a cruel and incomprehensible irony.

Many people have asked me why my mother stayed with John DeMoulas in such a complicated and ultimately desperate relationship. I certainly have no answer, nor does my mother, but I cannot bring myself to let my anger mitigate my love for her. She was and is the victim of lies told to her and lies she told to herself. She believed those lies because they represented her only hope for survival. Part of me wants to believe that my mother was deeply in love with John DeMoulas all those years and that she was truly blind because of that love. Clearly, she was desperate for his attention and affection, if that's the right word to describe what he gave her during their relationship.

Their relationship lasted for nearly fourteen years, until my mother was in her midthirties and my father was in his late fifties. Perhaps my father had affairs over that same period, or perhaps he was faithful to both his wife and his mistress. Regardless, he must have found something in my mother that he wanted to hold on to; maybe it was nothing more complicated than her love and her passion for him. Whatever held them together, fourteen years is a long time—fourteen years fueled by alcohol, loneliness, and, given the staggering consequences, remarkable degrees of self-indulgence on the part of both my father and my mother. I choose to believe what I think a lot of children of divorced or illegitimate parents believe, or want to believe, as they grow older: on the night I was conceived, it was out of love. It might not be true, but it is what I choose to believe.

Toward the end of my mother and father's relationship, it was obvious to all of us that they fought more and spoke less. He was spending less time running his liquor stores and more time at his vacation homes in New Hampshire and Florida. In those later years, when there was no longer any pretext of any meaningful relationship, my father rarely called my mother or stopped by our apartment building. When he did pull up outside in his big black Cadillac, he'd honk the horn, and my mother would send one of us down to pick up a bag of groceries or, occasionally, small amounts of cash. Eventually, he slowly faded away and out of our lives.

As I've said, though, the final fading away did not happen all at once. It was a gradual process. As my siblings and I grew older, we rebelled against life and figures of authority. I suppose that was natural, given our dire circumstances. My brother Mike got into trouble as a teenager. A woman we knew only as Mrs. Brown arrived at the police station or the courthouse to straighten things out.

There were also a number of DeMoulas family couriers whom, from time to time, used to deliver small amounts of cash to us. But the money only appeared when Uncle Mike thought the risk of exposure was especially great. Usually, that meant one of my brothers had threatened to talk publicly about our father. It gradually became clear to us that Uncle Mike, not our father, was making the decisions where the Bedard family was concerned. One time, Uncle Mike sent my mother a check for $800 through one of his emissaries, and due to the large amount of the check, we all hoped that this gesture might signal a newfound commitment to our welfare.

We were wrong.

Shortly thereafter, we realized his overture was nothing more than what we all came to recognize as a gift of silence—a gift to ensure we would make no attempt to sully the good DeMoulas name. These types of gestures were nothing more than an offensive in a complex game of emotional blackmail. When I was about thirteen, Uncle Mike called my brothers and sisters and me to the DeMoulas warehouse. He told my mother he wanted to "get a good look at us all together." He'd never seen us all at once. I am convinced that he wanted to see if there was a family resemblance, and of course, there was! My siblings and I all have Mediterranean complexions. We look as Greek as they come. When we got there, he pulled us into his office, where no one could see us, and handed us each fifty dollars. Then he said, and I'll never forget the menacing tone in his voice, "Now forget about your father. Come to me when you need something."

We watched him as he walked away. We just stood there looking at each other, and then we walked back to the car and drove back to the housing projects.

When things got really desperate, my mother made one of us go see Uncle Mike. Mostly, he turned us down with nothing more than a wave of his hand. Generally, we were asking for money to buy food. One time, I went to see my father because I needed a pair of glasses, and he said, "Just tape them—they are fine," and then he laughed. I will never forget that.

In time, something prompted Uncle Mike to realize that he and his family couldn't totally ignore us. The DeMoulases had to exert some degree of control over us or run the risk of us sharing our dirty little secret with someone. So one by one, Uncle Mike offered my brothers and sisters jobs, either at the warehouse or in one of the

Lowell stores. We did our jobs like any employee, but in the back of my mind, I always resented the fact that we would never share in the vast wealth of the family we were serving. Did we have a right to some the fortune? I think we did insofar as John should have shouldered the responsibility for our upbringing and education.

Naturally, John was of a different opinion. In some ways, Uncle Mike was more in tune with our needs than our own father was. Uncle Mike was looking out for the family name, but giving us jobs still helped, at least a little. It also spurred within me a sense of utter despair and confusion. I could not understand why our lives were so bad when, with just a little common decency, they could have been much better.

Later, I spiraled out of control, sinking into drug addiction to the point where my entire life was all about feeding my habit. I lived on the streets. My body deteriorated, as did my mind. I lived in a vortex of misery. Had my father seen me, he would have called me a bum and walked away, turning his back on the desperate man he'd sired many years ago with a woman he seduced with his good looks and boyish charm.

FIVE

School became increasingly difficult for me; I couldn't seem to focus on anything I read or on anything my teachers said. I also had trouble seeing the blackboard. I knew something was wrong with my eyes, but I never had enough money to buy myself a new pair of glasses.

I now know that I have suffered and continue to suffer from what is clinically known as attention-deficit/hyperactivity disorder, or ADHD. The principal characteristics of this disease are inattention, hyperactivity, and impulsivity—all personality traits familiar to me. According to the experts, and I quote from the letter I received from the Massachusetts Health Department in July of 1994,

> ADHD is a condition that becomes apparent in the early school years and it is hard for children with ADHD to control their behavior and to pay attention. Children with ADHD face a difficult but not insurmountable task ahead. In order to achieve their

full potential, they should receive help, guidance, and understanding from parents, guidance counselors, and the public education system.

Clearly, those in a position to help me during my abbreviated school experience were not aware of this condition. Or if they were, they were unprepared or uninterested in dealing with it—with me.

My brothers and sisters all had similar problems in school. There was no such thing as a program for children with special needs in the Lowell school system back then. So for all of us, school was just a place to be during the day; no one ever expected anything of any of us.

At the end of my sophomore year, when I was fifteen, Mr. Jones, the principal, called me into his office.

"George," he said, "it's not going to do you any good to stay in school anymore. You're not smart enough to make it. Why don't you just quit and go get a job? That would be the best thing for you."

That was all he said. I received no explanation as to why he, my teachers, and the system were giving up on me—no words of encouragement and no sympathy. He gave me nothing except the sense that I wasn't worth their time anymore. It was that simple. I was so unhappy in school that the idea of going off on my own appealed to me.

So I quit.

Not seeing that I had any other choice, I went to my uncle Mike and asked him for a job. This was the first time I'd done this, though eventually, all my brothers and sisters would find work in the warehouse or stores. He hired me to work as a bagger at the

DeMoulas Supermarket on Dummer Street. It was 1976. At the time, my mother was working as a barmaid and was out most nights.

I arrived at the store on the first day, saw my uncle, and said, "Hello, Uncle Mike."

He pulled me quickly aside and said, "From now on, you will call me Mr. D. Don't you ever call me Uncle, and don't talk to anyone else. You understand me? If you need something, you come to me."

I soon realized that none of the other employees would acknowledge me. I didn't know what they thought of me or who they thought I was, but they knew that none of the bosses ever talked to me. I also know they saw the holes in my boots. So if the rumors were true and I really was a DeMoulas, none of the pieces fit. I walked to the store every day and walked home alone in the evening. I didn't earn a lot of money, and I seriously doubt my brothers and sisters and I were paid as much as the other people doing our same jobs. I was able to buy food each week with my paycheck, but not much more.

I had little contact with kids my age, and I felt isolated. I was also confronting my own sexuality more openly, realizing that I was gay. I started spending time with much older people. I felt comfortable with them. They somehow understood me better than my peers did. They somehow knew me better than I knew myself.

Eventually, when I was about eighteen or nineteen, I left the Dummer Street store and went to work at the warehouse where my uncles Mike and George had their offices. My father also had an office there, and sometimes he'd make an appearance. I always thought it was curious that none of the offices ever had a sign indicating whose office it was. The atmosphere was like some kind of secret DeMoulas society. My job was building pallets. All day long, I'd load wooden pallets with orders to be shipped out to the various stores, and then I'd load the pallets onto an eighteen-wheeler. It was demanding work.

Once I began working at the warehouse, I couldn't walk back and forth to work; it was too far. So I bought an old Ford Maverick for $800. At about the same time, one of Uncle George's daughters, my half cousin, turned sixteen, and her parents bought her a Porsche. That was when I started to notice the cars my half brothers, sisters, and cousins were driving. I began to realize that this family that was my family but not really my family was wealthy beyond anything I'd ever imagined.

Although my father was not directly involved in the DeMoulas Supermarket operations, he had the package-store franchise. Every time a new DeMoulas market came online, my father opened a liquor store in the same plaza, and by then, he was spending all of his time running that profitable business.

The Golden Nugget had burned in a fire, and Marion's Café, where my parents had met, had also closed. Whenever my father and I saw each other at the warehouse, he rarely acknowledged me; he pretended to be preoccupied so that he could avoid me.

I think I knew from the beginning that my brothers and sisters and I were in dead-end jobs. Uncle Mike was only doing what he had to do to keep us under his control. It didn't matter how hard we worked—he was never going to give any of us real responsibility, because that might raise questions about who we were.

My brothers John and Mike became increasingly bitter about how they were being treated at the warehouse and the circumstances under which they were living their lives. They decided to confront Mr. D.

I don't know what they expected, but soon thereafter, they were let go. I suppose to his credit, Uncle Mike gave them each a little money to start their own businesses, one a roofing company and the other a drywall company.

Was it hush money? Was it guilt money? I don't know. Perhaps it was both.

As with so much about my uncle Mike, it was hard to know the truth. I do know that protecting the DeMoulas family, its reputation, and its business was always his first and only priority. Indeed, he had already made a series of business and personal decisions that, years later, would lead to his downfall.

In the end, my brothers and sisters and I were not Uncle Mike's responsibility. We were not his children. Although, over the years, he did more for us than our own father, we all wavered between hating him and trying to stay in his good graces.

I was still living with my mother in the projects and my younger sister, Patricia. She was still in high school in those years and was the only one of us who would finish high school.

Had my brothers and sisters and I just been poor, I think we might have done better, but we weren't just poor. We lived our lives with the constant reminder of the special circumstances into which we had been born. All we had to do was witness the lives our half brothers, sisters, and cousins were living. They drove expensive cars, wore new clothes, and had plenty of cash in their pockets.

That made us confused and angry.

I worked at the warehouse for about six years, and it was during those years that I became heavily involved in drugs and alcohol. It was obvious, even to those who didn't know me, that I was gay. For some reason, my brother John told Uncle Mike I was gay, and after that, Uncle Mike seemed even more reluctant to deal with me.

I had enough. The constant talking behind my back, the jokes about my sexuality, the obvious contempt my uncle and father had for me, and the certainty that there was no future for me in the family business finally drove me to a long-overdue decision.

I went to Uncle Mike and told him I was quitting. As he had with my older brothers, he gave me money to start my own business. I of course intended to thank him, but I never had a chance. When he handed me a check for $7,500, it was if he were finally being relieved of a great burden. He said, "Here's the check. Take it and leave, and don't ever come back."

Although I knew I had made the right decision, I was afraid. I was suddenly cut loose from the only place I had ever worked and, in some bizarre way, the only real security I had ever known.

I started a cleaning business that I called Economy Cleaning Service. After working by myself for several months, I had acquired a number of customers, and I began hiring people to work with me. Since I was used to living hand to mouth, I was able to run the business on a shoestring. I had to because I was spending what little profit the business was generating on crack cocaine.

Drugs and alcohol were distractions that would cost me several years of my life.

SIX

I've thought a great deal about why I abused drugs, and I've learned a great deal about myself in recent years through the professional counseling I've sought. I've also learned that people with ADHD often become addicted to drugs because the drugs calm the pain they are suffering. I suspect my descent into one of the darkest times of my life resulted from a combination of factors, my childhood and the ADHD ranking among the most salient. My addiction to drugs began when I was working at the warehouse, and the addiction became more serious when I was out on my own. I managed to get up every morning and go to work, but I had to supplement my income by shoplifting.

In short order, I lost my cleaning business and myself to drugs. Some days, my only food was other people's leftovers. My world was closing down around me. Every day, I moved closer to a kind of life-altering experience—the kind of experience that, like having a prison record hung around your neck, makes it nearly impossible to ever start over with a clean slate.

You can't simply leave behind some things that happen to you in life. Some things chase you down the street until they grab you by the ankles and pull you down hard and fast right into the gutter. That's exactly what happened to me, and I was lucky enough to eventually find the inner strength I needed to pull myself back up again. Part of the courage came from a deep desire to at last vindicate my mother and to claim my rightful name. The quest breathed new resolve into my reality. I channeled the deep-seated anger I felt at the injustice my siblings, my mother, and I suffered at the hands of the DeMoulas family into a drive to right the wrongs of the past. As was the case with most of my brothers and sisters, I could no longer escape the realities of my life. What happened to us during those years of our childhood and early adulthood, in many ways, cemented our fates—for some of us, forever.

We had no role models, no one to guide us. So we had to make up our own rules as we went along, often with disastrous results. Being gay can lead to a lonely and isolated life, which was the way it was for me growing up. There was no structure in my life, and I never felt I belonged. Being gay and outside of the mainstream of life seems right to me. Quite simply, I know the gay community is where I now belong, but it took me many years to fully accept myself for who I was. I have compassion, and I identify with taking care of people. Whenever the broken wing comes to my door, I respond in whatever way is appropriate. But when someone is kind or gives me something, I don't know how to react. If someone were to ever tell me he loved me and wanted to be with me, I'd be incapable of believing him.

My father, the Greek, could have helped turn things around for me if only he'd had the decency and the heart to do so. It wouldn't have taken much for him to give me a sense of my own worth while I was growing up. In many ways, I don't think he had much of a sense of his own self-worth. You can't treat people the way he did and still feel you are worth something, that you are worthy of all of life's great gifts. I do think he loved himself more than he loved any other human being, but I also think he was insecure and cruel. He could have helped, but he failed me. I had to find my sense of self-worth somewhere else.

At the age of twenty-six, I was in a downward spiral, and I realized my life was out of control. I decided to get help for my drug and alcohol addiction—the year was 1988. I started by making numerous phone calls, hoping to be accepted into a rehabilitation facility. Days later, I received a return call from Quincy Detox in Quincy, Massachusetts. They had accepted me, and so my journey to put myself back together began in earnest. Within one hour after that phone call, my sister Dorothy and I were driving from my mother's apartment in Lowell to the detox facility in Quincy.

Upon my arrival, a nurse performed a physical on me and then sent me to my shared bedroom. I felt desperate to save my own life. I went to three meetings a day for twenty-eight days, which was the maximum allowance for free care. My days started at 7:00 a.m. with a bowl of cereal, followed by our morning meeting at 8:00 a.m. Between meetings, we had free time to use the gym, read a book, or watch TV, but for me, it was time to reevaluate my life and find out who I truly was, which I'm certain most other people were doing as well.

We had midday meetings followed by evening meetings, and so it was every day for those twenty-eight days. Knowing that those twenty-eight days would end, I had to realize that I would have to reenter society and be able to use the tools the program had given me.

On my last day of treatment, I awoke before sunrise. I felt excited, but most of all, I had an overwhelming feeling of fear. That morning, as I was packing my bag, a nurse entered my room and asked if I was ready to leave; she told me my ride was there. At that moment, I knew I was about to become the person I was supposed to be. I fought back my fears, which were entirely justified. Addicts relapse all the time. Wanting to find the courage to change isn't the same as actually doing it. I told the nurse that I was ready to leave, that I was starting a new chapter in my life. She smiled and sent me on my way, and I haven't looked back since.

I returned to my mother's apartment in Lowell, where I would begin my aftercare treatment, which included attending ninety meetings in ninety days. During my aftercare, I started to call my old clients from my cleaning company in hopes of re-creating my cleaning business. At the time, I was completely broke; I did not even have a bank account. All of the clients I called welcomed me back with open arms and believed in me more than I believed in myself. Gradually, my self-confidence grew. Positive feedback can do wonders for a lost soul. It can create its own energy. It can help you turn yourself around.

I drove to the clients' houses in my used 1983 black Monte Carlo with a mop, bucket, and cleaning supplies that my mother had given me from her apartment. In the process, I was able to start rebuilding my business.

During my first year of sobriety, I smothered myself in AA meetings and work. I was able to rent a small seven-hundred-square-foot apartment in the Drum Hill section of Lowell. It wasn't much, but I had earned it.

Over the next nine years, I stayed sober and kept the cleaning company running. At that point, I was a bit more financially stable and able to rent an apartment in a better neighborhood in Tyngsboro, Massachusetts.

At that apartment, I had dinner parties for fellow AA members. I had converted the one-car garage into the dining room, and noticing this, one of my dinner guests said to me that I was in the wrong business and that I should be decorating homes, not cleaning them. That comment sparked my interest in researching interior design.

After researching and applying for wholesale and resale certificates, I was able to open Creative Touch Interiors in 1997, but much happened before then. The DeMoulas family was about to implode.

SEVEN

My uncle George DeMoulas, whom my mother named me after, died of a heart attack on June 27, 1971, while in Greece on a holiday with his family. He was fifty-one and left behind his wife, Evanthea, and their four children: Diana, Arthur T., Evan, and Fotene.

I was nine.

Uncle George was the one member of the DeMoulas family who, I believe, had true compassion for my family and me and understood our plight. Many times, he sent over groceries from the nearby DeMoulas market. Perhaps had he not died, our lives might have turned out differently. Uncle Mike was the dominant brother, at least when it came to the business. My father stood in the background, just as George did. When George died, his death left a power vacuum in the family hierarchy—one that proved too tempting for my uncle to ignore. As he tortured us in dead-end jobs in the family business, intimidating us into silence and essentially doing the dirty work of his brother John, my uncle was in the process of stabbing his own family in the back.

The implosion of the DeMoulas family actually began in 1964, when I was just three years old. My uncles George and Mike met to sign each other's will, which named each other the executor of the other's estate. During that meeting, they also apparently solemnly vowed to assume responsibility for each other's family upon the death of the other and agreed to equally divide the business between the families.

At the time, my uncles were on the verge of becoming far wealthier than Athas and Efrosine ever could have imagined when they opened that first DeMoulas Market on Dummer Street in 1917.

When Uncle George died, Uncle Mike established trust funds for George's four children. The trust funds would provide the children with annual incomes of $25,000 until they reached the age of thirty. Mike began expanding the business. His first move was to buy an existing supermarket from the Grand Union chain. The supermarket was located in Salem, New Hampshire, and it was less than quarter of a mile away from an existing DeMoulas Supermarket. So Mike changed the name of his new acquisition to Market Basket, a new brand name he was to give to every supermarket the chain opened thereafter.

Uncle Mike's decision to establish a separate, distinct brand would later be characterized in a court of law as a critical strategic move underlying his plans to divert DeMoulas company assets into a corporation that he alone controlled.

After Uncle George's death, depending on how one viewed things, my uncle Mike either played the role of a caring and loving uncle to his nieces and nephews or was systemically and ruthlessly robbing each them of his or her equity stake in the DeMoulas Supermarket empire.

Most people, including several juries of his peers and the Commonwealth of Massachusetts, eventually came to recognize the second scenario as the truth: Uncle Mike was guilty of egregious, fraudulent behavior.

As the facts eventually proved, although it appeared he was fulfilling his solemn vow and legal responsibility to care for his brother's widow and children, Uncle Mike was plotting to deny them all of their rightful inheritances. Within a matter of days after George's death, Mike had his lawyer prepare documents that would accelerate the process.

All he required was the signature of George's wife, Evanthea. She signed the papers without question or hesitation.

According to Uncle George's son Arthur S. DeMoulas, six weeks after George's death, Uncle Mike began his move to consolidate the assets of the DeMoulas Supermarket chain within a new corporate structure that he named Market Basket. It wasn't until many years later, however, that the deception came to light, but much to my delight, it did all come out eventually.

Both George's wife, Evanthea, and another of his sons, Evan, had been appointed to serve on the company's board of directors, but in 1980, Mike had Evanthea dismissed from the board. He claimed she was having an affair with a married man, which made her unsuitable to represent her family's interests.

In late 1989, one year after I got clean and sober, Evan was asked to sign some papers associated with what he was told was to be a routine tax audit of the sale of some of his stock. Evan knew he had never authorized any sale of his stock and refused to sign the documents. His suspicions aroused, Evan and his family contacted a lawyer and began to dig beneath the surface for proof of Uncle Mike's malfeasance.

Prior to George's death, he and his brother Mike had owned the DeMoulas corporation as equal partners. Twenty years later, Mike and his children controlled 100 percent of the real estate and 84 percent of the stock.

From an early age, George DeMoulas's children had been signing documents prepared for them by their father or by their uncle Mike. They had absolute faith in their uncle and, after their father's death, trusted the man closest to them to continue to care for them both financially and emotionally.

After an audit of the corporate books, the accountants George's family had hired to investigate the fraud issued a lengthy report of their findings. The report showed that over the course of two decades, Uncle Mike had been helping himself to the assets in George's estate—assets that rightfully belonged to his widow and children.

A lawsuit was filed on April 5, 1990, alleging that Mike had defrauded George's family out of what the auditors determined might be as much as $800 million. By that time, Uncle Mike's stock holdings in the company had climbed to 92 percent. The remaining 8 percent was still in George's son Arthur's name, but George's other heirs had lost all of their shares.

At some point over the next several years, the two families stopped talking to each other altogether.

When Uncle George's son Evan died in an automobile accident in 1993, Uncle Mike and his family learned of his death through their attorneys, who told them not to attend the funeral.

I do not know for certain if my father had any involvement in the dispute or took sides. I do know that when he and several family members arrived for the wake, they were turned away.

After numerous delays, the trial against Uncle Mike began in the early 1990s in Middlesex Superior Court in Cambridge, Massachusetts. It was the first of six lawsuits and one appeal.

Ironically, I was about to begin waging my own legal battle against the DeMoulas family.

I was thirty-three.

EIGHT

As Uncle Mike battled with George's family, I launched my own litigation. I wanted John to acknowledge that I was his son. I wasn't suing for money. I only wanted him to admit to the fact that my mother had been his mistress for fourteen years, the affair had resulted in five children, and he'd done nothing whatsoever to ensure that we had food, shelter, and clothing. By odd coincidence, during the first trial, I was often at the same courthouse, attending to my own affairs.

On many days, I'd stand in the back of the courtroom and watch while attorneys representing the George DeMoulas family made allegations of gross misconduct against Mike DeMoulas and his immediate family.

Standing there, I was a silent witness to what I can describe only as emotional carnage.

During that first trial, my uncle Mike was on the stand for seventeen days. At one point during his testimony, his son Arthur T. became so upset that he charged at our cousin Arthur S., George's son, and punched him in the face. After some pushing, shoving, and swearing, the two cousins were separated. The trial continued the next day with extra security, an admonition from the judge.

The jury deliberated for thirteen days and, on May 26, 1994, ruled in favor of the plaintiffs (George DeMoulas's family). The judge ordered Uncle Mike to return stock estimated to be worth something on the order of half a billion dollars to Uncle George's family and give the family control of 51 percent of the company.

Uncle Mike appealed these rulings, but ultimately, the Supreme Judicial Court of Massachusetts upheld them.

Over the course of the 1990s, five more trials took place, several of which were ongoing at the same time. One was a contempt trial against Uncle Mike for transferring $68 million in additional company assets to his own name after the courts had frozen the assets. Other trials involved charges that Uncle Mike continued to move assets from DeMoulas to Market Basket and improperly managed the company's pension funds. There were two trials in which Uncle Mike accused Uncle George's family of wiretapping the company headquarters.

Throughout these years of proceedings, a number of incidents occurred that I can describe only as bordering on the bizarre.

In one instance, a juror contacted a member of Uncle Mike's family and offered to change his vote in return for a payoff of $220,000. He was ultimately discovered, and the FBI arrested him.

Another series of events that provided ample fodder for the local tabloids involved Mike's lawyers allegedly paying a stripper and acknowledged drug addict half a million dollars to meet with a former boyfriend of one of George's daughters and get him to admit he had been involved in the wiretapping scheme. All I know is that the jury in that trial didn't fall for that story.

And then there were Uncle Mike's constant assertions throughout the years that the judge, Maria Lopez, who presided over two of the cases, was biased against him. As was ultimately revealed, he and three of his prominent attorneys would go to great lengths to prove those assertions.

The lawyers, including Richard K. Donahgue, a former advisor to John F. Kennedy and the former president of Nike Corporation, concocted an elaborate scheme to bribe the judge's law clerk, Paul Walsh, into discrediting Judge Lopez.

According to the charges, the lawyers created a fake international insurance company and invited Walsh to job interviews in New York and Canada. During those interviews with a representative of the alleged insurance company, the representative secretly taped Walsh as he asked questions; the lawyers hoped Walsh's answers would show bias on the part of the judge toward George DeMoulas's family.

When the clerk discovered the plan, he went to the FBI and agreed to assist that agency in unearthing the plot. He succeeded, and the three lawyers were brought before the State Board of Overseers on charges. They were later found guilty.

In yet another final twist to the story, Judge Lopez resigned from the bench in 2003 over allegations that she'd mishandled a case involving the sexual assault of a child. I am told she believes that allies of Mike DeMoulas orchestrated much of the uproar over that case.

Judge Lopez now has her own reality show on Court TV.

Those lawsuits took more than ten years to resolve. As a result, the Michael and George DeMoulas families now have the distinction of being responsible for what proved to be the lengthiest, most expensive civil litigation in the history of the Commonwealth of Massachusetts.

And throughout it all, I had many questions.

What on earth had motivated my uncle Mike to defraud his brother George and his brother George's family? By everyone's account, the two brothers had an excellent relationship, and Mike certainly had acquired his own substantial wealth.

The only answer appears to be the obvious answer: good old-fashioned greed.

How was it possible that Uncle Mike thought his deception, in so many ways and over so many years, would escape detection? He was a smart and savvy businessman and certainly had to understand that—somehow, somewhere—someone was going to rip down the curtain and expose him for his flagrant and fraudulent behavior.

What does it say about someone when he amasses enormous wealth and power and then turns around and abuses that power? The consequences of what my uncle Mike did and the destruction he wrought are almost impossible to believe.

I know the wounds of the DeMoulas family remain to this day, and they will never heal.

My uncle Telemachus "Mike" Arthur DeMoulas died in 2002. He was eighty-two.

While the DeMoulas family members were preparing for their initial battle in court, I was preparing for a legal battle of my own. I was formulating a plan to change my legal name to George Arthur DeMoulas and to amend my birth certificate accordingly. Although they had a great deal to lose, and despite the distractions they were facing, I was quite certain that the DeMoulas family, including my father, would respond to my decision to fight for my rightful name with all of the considerable resources available to them.

They were suffering from extraordinary degrees of unflattering publicity as a result of the ongoing litigation between my uncle Mike and my uncle George's family. The last thing the family needed or wanted was more negative publicity. They all also knew that the social climate had changed dramatically since my mother had taken my father to court in the 1960s. Deadbeat fathers were now being hunted down and hauled off to jail for failing to support their children. Society no longer viewed women as bearing sole responsibility for having children out of wedlock, and these mothers were eliciting greater degrees of sympathy both in the public eye and in the courts. Whether their children were legitimate or not, fathers were no longer innocent bystanders but were equally accountable.

On another level, the DeMoulas family business catered overwhelmingly to women, and the family feared a significant number of them might decide to stop patronizing their local Market Basket when they learned of the impoverished lives led by five children born out of wedlock to the eldest DeMoulas son, my father, John.

I also suspect the DeMoulases understood it was going to be difficult to prove that I wasn't my father's son. Nothing could change the fact that I bore a startling resemblance to my uncle George DeMoulas.

Nevertheless, the DeMoulas family made the decision to enter the fray, and just as I had expected, the DeMoulas machine proved to be formidable.

As the trials revealed, the DeMoulas family had amassed an astonishing fortune. This wealth translated into considerable influence in legal and political circles, both in Lowell and in Boston.

And the DeMoulases were determined to squash the unfavorable publicity that would certainly result from my court action.

I knew I would need to find an attorney who was willing to go up against the DeMoulas family and risk the potential backlash. I also prepared myself for the fact that they would use any tactic at their disposal to stall until I had exhausted my funds and my will to continue to fight the battle.

I also assumed my father and my uncle Mike would attempt to settle the case the old-fashioned way.

On several occasions during the run-up to the trial and the nearly seven years of legal maneuverings that followed, they asked me how much money it would take to make me go away.

One afternoon, I unexpectedly ran into my uncle Mike in Lowell. "George," he said, "take the fifty thousand dollars we've offered you, and stop this nonsense. You'll never win, and it will be the fastest fifty thousand dollars you'll ever make."

As always, I declined.

None of them ever seemed to understand that some things cannot be bought, no matter how much money is thrown at the problem. I also came to realize that none of the DeMoulas family had any real understanding of how my mother, my brothers and sisters, and I had suffered economically, socially, and emotionally as a result of the way we were treated.

Or perhaps they simply didn't care.

Within a week of that confrontation with my uncle Mike, I was thrown out of the house he had been renting to me in an attempt to retain some control over my life. Although I understood his motives, I was so desperate at the time that it was all I could afford.

The day after I left, the house was bulldozed to the ground, and the plot of land remains vacant to this day.

At the outset of the proceedings, my father and Uncle Mike hired a lawyer, Monroe Inker, to represent the family. Inker was one of the most powerful family lawyers in the city of Boston, and the DeMoulases instructed him and his associates to crush the case as quickly as possible.

As the proceedings finally got under way, a number of factors worked in my favor.

After I fired my first attorney, who was unable to break through the legal stalemates thrown our way during the first months I pursued the case, I hired an aggressive attorney from Boston, Ellen Poster.

Someone I trusted had referred me to her, and for reasons still not entirely clear to me, she agreed to take the case. Once she became involved, she seemed convinced, at least on most days, that I had a fighting chance.

Also, the DeMoulases had underestimated the amount of time, energy, and financial resources the ongoing trials between the DeMoulas factions would take. Those trials destroyed the united front that would have been useful in creating a barrier to my success.

I was clearly a distraction but certainly not at the level that the potential loss of billions of dollars in present and future earnings presented to both sides. In a real sense, the greed of my uncle Mike laid the foundation for my ultimate victory.

NINE

No one on their side counted on one thing: more than anything, I wanted my rightful name. In many ways, my life depended on winning the case. The desire for justice had helped me get clean and sober and stay that way even when things got tough for me in business and in my personal life. I felt driven. I felt as if my life had meaning, as if I had a purpose. Losing the case would have been like losing a part of myself. I was never prepared to imagine what it would be like to lose the case, and on many days, I wavered between despair and hope. I worked just to keep up with the legal costs required to keep the case before the courts, never sure how I would pay my other bills. The legal battle was all-consuming.

I did not know—and could not have known—just how overwhelming the experience would actually be. Some days, after meeting with my attorney or spending a day in court, I'd have to pull my car over to the side of the road and compose myself. On many days, I questioned my resolve and my sanity.

I am sure there were days when their side believed they would win; after all, they had might on their side. There are thousands of lawsuits filed each year that the little guy looses to the big guns and big money. In those instances, truth is irrelevant.

Closure has become an overused word these days, but for me, it represents an interesting emotional current that runs through the lives of those who suffer and lose someone or something that is irreplaceable. While I can never fully recover from the horrors of my childhood, I could get the one thing that made me their equal—my last name—and closure of sorts.

Am I vindictive? I am, but only at times. My name was the one thing I asked for, and they refused to give it to me. I would have to beat it out of them through the legal system, and if I succeeded, it would be a win beyond anything I could imagine.

It would be a real-life David-and-Goliath story.

People who don't know me well assumed then and assume now that I was after their money. With the exception of the meager handouts I received as a child and the $7,500 Uncle Mike gave me when I left the DeMoulas warehouse, I have never taken a cent from the DeMoulas family.

Through all the years of anguish and humiliation, the one thing the DeMoulases could laud over me was that I was not really a DeMoulas. On one occasion, I went to see my cousin Arthur T. to ask for financial help. He told me, "I can't help every stranger who comes begging to me for money; you don't belong here," and then he turned his back on me. I'll never forget the anger and sadness I felt at the way he dismissed me. That meeting went a long way in provoking me to fight with ferocity for my case. I knew in my head and my heart who I truly was.

They could brush me aside, dismiss me, and look down on me as white trash, but my having the legal right to assume the DeMoulas name, at least on the surface, would change everything.

Or at least it would change everything in my view, and that was what counted.

The first hurdle was to get the courts to agree to a pretrial hearing. I was usually on the left side of the courtroom, and they were on the right. I had one lawyer. Often, three or four lawyers represented them. If the situation hadn't been so serious, it might have been comical. To any bystander, it would have seemed that the odds were firmly tilted against me.

In the judgment of my attorney, Ellen Poster, our best hope of establishing paternity and my right to the DeMoulas name was to submit into evidence the decades-old court orders pertaining to my mother's attempts to receive child support. Although the amendment of my birth certificate was all I was concerned with, I approved her strategy.

Once the child-support issue came to the fore, my father's lawyers attempted to connect it with any legal rights I might eventually claim with regard to my father's estate.

As stated in the court records, the primary defense was that there had to be "adequate reason for seeking determination of paternity." My father's lawyers argued that we could not bring an action against a living person with regard to his estate.

"There are no rights to inheritance while the father is alive. And if such determination were made during the father's lifetime, it could easily be negated by a specific omission in the will, therefore giving no meaning to such determination."

My father's attorneys also argued that seeking past child support should not be considered for "an emancipated (legal adult) child born out of wedlock." They went on to claim that there is "no rationale to award past child support to an emancipated child. Such a result would be unjust enrichment and would serve no purpose."

I was concerned that my father's attempts to muddy my intentions might prove to be a successful tactic, but we responded by offering the following evidence from the initial suit brought by my mother for child support: "Defendant was found guilty on February 13, 1963 in the District Court of Lowell of non support of plaintiff George A. Bedard and his siblings, all of whom were born out of wedlock to the Plaintiff Dorothy M. Bedard and the Defendant." At the same time Ellen Poster was working her way through the laborious and highly complex court proceedings, I was searching for something, a piece of evidence that would confirm that my birthfather's name was indisputably John DeMoulas.

By chance, I picked up a copy of the *Lowell Sun* one afternoon and stumbled across an article about the closing of Shaw Hospital, where I had been born. After detailing the long history of the hospital, the article mentioned that that the hospital was planning to provide copies of medical records to interested parties the next day.

My mother and I were on the front steps of the hospital at 7:30 a.m. the following morning, waiting for the doors to open. As we delved through the records, we discovered a critical document—perhaps the only legal document other than the court records pertaining to the child-support hearings that would tie my family and me to the DeMoulases.

It was a simple statement on a flimsy piece of paper that my mother had written in her hand shortly after my sister Melveen was born almost forty years earlier.

The statement read, "I Dorothy Bedard and John DeMoulas will let the people named on legal papers take my baby daughter."

My mother did not remember writing the note. She did remember, however, that the process that had led to my older sister's adoption had taken place without the proper legal releases. So this hastily written note was, to her knowledge, the only link that tied her and John DeMoulas together as parents of that child.

Shortly before noon on that same day, the hospital administrator suddenly closed the doors to the hospital and issued a statement to the effect that no more records would be available to former patients.

I have no way of knowing, but I believe now, as I did then, that the only explanation for this sudden decision was that the DeMoulases somehow intervened.

If they were, in fact, responsible for the administrator's abrupt decision, they were too late.

I had what I needed. Fate had intervened on my side.

Although I understood that finding this key piece of evidence might prove critically important to my case, I remained convinced that I would need more conclusive proof in a court of law that John DeMoulas was my father.

That proof would have to be in the form of a DNA test, which was rapidly becoming the tool for truth in courtrooms across the country. The problem was how to get John to submit to one. At the moment, the answer to that vexing question remained unclear.

TEN

Midway through the court proceedings, Monroe Inker, my father's attorney, pulled me aside. He and the DeMoulases were now aware we were going to fight for the right to subject my father to DNA testing, and they all knew there would be no winning that round.

Inker said, "We will admit that you are John's son," but he also said, "You are not going to get anything, so what's the point of continuing to press this matter?"

I responded with a simple statement: "I just want my rightful name and to be recognized as John DeMoulas's son."

He kept saying, "Why? For what reason? Do you want money? You will never be what they are. You will never be in their class. Your father is sick, and he's not going to live forever. When he dies, we will cremate his body, and that will be the end of this DNA business—and that will be the end of your case. John does not want to go through this with you."

"I want my name," I repeated over and over.

Once again, they proceeded with the delaying tactics. My uncle Mike and the rest of the family were hoping my father, who had liver cancer, would die before the case went to trial. They would destroy his body, and I would never get my rightful name.

They were wrong.

During the course of these lengthy pretrial motions, something interesting took place that led me to believe I had finally succeeded in getting their attention, at least on one level.

On June 18, 1998, Monroe Inker, his associate Melissa A. Gallivan, and the firm of White, Inker, Aronson, PC, withdrew the representation as counsel for the defendant, my father, John DeMoulas.

In their motion to withdraw, the lawyers informed the judge that "a significant disagreement [had] arisen between them and the defendant" and that the defendant had asked them to "withdraw their appearance."

I always felt there were several reasons for this turn of events.

Monroe Inker was a well-known attorney, and his involvement in my case was drawing far more attention to the matter than my father had anticipated. Also, I am certain the family was pressuring my father to give in to my demands and settle the matter rather than risk further public exposure and embarrassment.

However, without the benefit of a financial settlement, which I had repeatedly refused, my father was standing firm in his decision to prevent me from taking his name.

Meanwhile, my father had seemingly disappeared off the face of the earth.

His new attorney, Sheldon Ganz, continued to press the courts to dismiss the case on the same basis: that we had failed to provide grounds to claim back child support.

At the same time, we had been thwarted at every turn in our attempts to serve my father with the legal documents that would compel him to answer the pleadings. Over a period of several months, we had made considerable efforts to serve my father with the relevant papers. The sheriffs had made repeated visits to his home in Florida, where he was living most of the time; his house in New Hampshire; and the DeMoulas warehouse in Tewksbury, Massachusetts.

Without his response to our claims, the case could not be marked up for trial. This had been one of my father's lawyers' most effective delaying tactics.

One such failed attempt showed the lengths to which my father was prepared to go to rebuff my efforts to claim my rightful name. On November 4, 1997, my attorney gave the local deputy sheriff in Palm Beach County, Florida, this description of my father: "(John Demoulas) is 5'3", balding with gray hair. He walks slightly hunched over. He is 85 years of age but looks younger than his years. He smokes a cigar. He wears glasses."

The deputy sheriff, Mr. Ippollito, went to my father's house to serve the summons and subsequently submitted the following written report:

> Sitting in the yard, was a white male, approximately 80 years of age, short in stature, balding gray hair, glasses and smoking a cigar. He stated that his name was Michael Plain. He refused to show me any type of ID. Since the subject fit description which I was

provided for John Demoulas and I was aware that he may attempt to avoid service, I served him the documents.

Even at his advanced age, with debilitating cancer, my father was able to summon up the chutzpah to avoid service and to attempt to thwart the process.

The court battle had now become a true battle of wills. Even with all the legal intermediaries standing between my father and me, it ultimately had come down to just the two of us. Who, I wondered, was going to win that battle? I was determined that the winner would be me. It had become a point of honor. Also, I must admit that the vociferous protestations on his part made me want to proceed all the more just to spite him. He'd stuck it to me for decades, and now it was my turn to stick it to him. If he didn't want me to take his name so badly that he'd spend tens of thousands of dollars and stall for years, then by God, I'd see to it that I, not he, got the last laugh.

My attorney had filed the initial complaint on September 22, 1997, but it wasn't until eighteen months later, on April 14, 1999, that Edward F. Donnelly Jr., judge of the probate court, made the first significant ruling in the case.

In his ruling, he stated, "Authority of time to impose retroactive child support was eliminated. It is clear, however, that the original statute authorized child support." The judge further ruled that there comes "a point beyond which complaints for retroactive child support may not be brought."

But most importantly, the judge separated the child-support issue from my request to have my birth certificate amended.

He said, "The plaintiff's prayer for adjudication and amendment of the birth record may stand. The plaintiff has a legitimate interest in establishing paternity to protect whatever rights he may have under the law of descent."

The court was now willing to proceed with the case and hear testimony on the issue of my right to amend my birth certificate. For me, this was an extraordinary victory.

Moving forward, we focused all our efforts on securing the DNA evidence that would prove to the world once and for all that my claim to my rightful name was indeed valid.

My mother and I drove from Lowell to a courthouse in Cambridge to give our DNA samples. The procedure took place in the musty basement of the building, in a small area used for storing archival files. I helped my mother down several flights of stairs that, in some strange way, reminded me of the stairwells at the Bishop Markham housing projects in Lowell.

A representative of a company called Lab Corp was sitting at a desk with a folder in front of her. She was wearing a white starched jacket that seemed out of place with the surroundings. My mother and I sat down and filled out the necessary paperwork. The technician then carefully and gently swabbed the insides of our mouths and put the swabs containing our DNA into small plastic bags.

The Lab Corp representative sent our DNA to the lab that afternoon, and our part of the deal was sealed. Months later that same year, I won another victory. On October 4, 1999, Sheila E. McGovern, justice of the probate and family court, ruled that our motion for DNA testing be allowed. My father was to be compelled by court order to submit to testing.

After making her ruling, the judge looked down from the bench and said directly to me, "I thought there was no denying it. When I walked into the courtroom and saw you, I was almost embarrassed that we were even putting the legal system through this exercise."

Then she said to my father's lawyers, "There they are fighting over the big court case in the adjoining courtroom. I am disgusted. I know it's not about the money. They are fighting over millions of dollars, and they don't even want to give this man his name.

"I don't want to hear from your side anymore. Either he does the DNA, or George becomes his son. Swabbing is not painful. I don't care how sick your client is. There is no point in not going forth with the test. It will not hurt your client."

The ruling in the court document also contained an important statement that represented the second clear victory for me:

> If the Defendant fails to arrange for the taking of tissue samples so ordered or in the event of the defendants death, the court will draw adverse inference from said failure that the testing, if performed, would have yielded a statistical probability of paternity in excess of 97 percent that the defendant is the plaintiff's father.
>
> The court will, to the extent permissible by law, bar the defendant or his representative from adducing any evidence to the contrary at trial.

I had won the battle of wills.

If John DeMoulas submitted his DNA for testing, that would prove with absolute certainty he was my father. If he refused to submit his DNA, the court would rule that he was my father. It was now up to him to decide how to proceed.

He decided to keep his mouth shut, as it were.

Less than a month later, on November 1, 1999, the trial court of the probate and family court of the Commonwealth of Massachusetts made the following declarations:

1. John DeMoulas is the father of George A. Bedard.
2. George A. Bedard shall have the name of George A. DeMoulas.
3. The birth certificate shall be amended to state that his father is John DeMoulas and his name is George A. DeMoulas.
4. George A. DeMoulas has rights by descent to the estate of John DeMoulas.

I was in shock. In the end, it all happened quickly. Except for my attorney and my father's attorney, I was alone in the courtroom. My father's attorney didn't say a word. He gave me a cold a stare, turned on his heel, and walked out of the courtroom in defeat.

I immediately called my mother, who was living at an elderly housing facility in Lowell, and we both cried. I think for her, it meant that some of the mistakes she'd made when it came to John had finally been corrected. She knew she couldn't undo the damage done all those years ago—she knew it was too late for that—but she also knew that the family had been made to pay a price for what it did, however small it might have been. For me, the victories meant that I truly had delivered a hard slap to John and his family.

Now I'd have to get used to people calling me George DeMoulas. It had taken seven years of my life and thousands of dollars, but it was worth all the expense and anguish. I was, at long last, DeMoulas.

However, I was not about to let it end there.

I was determined to obtain John DeMoulas's DNA in order to prove before the world and beyond any doubt that he was my biological father. I also intended to preserve the rights of my siblings to make that same indisputable claim, and as luck would have it, I came out on top in the end. I showed my dad that I had the courage to stand strong against all odds and come out the winner in a fight he'd started long before I was even born.

ELEVEN

After the courts had ruled in my favor, I went to the DeMoulas warehouse and found my father, who had suddenly reappeared, sitting in his office. He was feeble and obviously sick. He was also unrelenting in his obvious disdain for me. He looked up at me from behind his desk and asked, "What do you people want from me?"

It was a hurt to last a lifetime. That was the last time I ever saw my father.

Within days after he was made aware of the court ruling, my father instructed his attorneys to ensure that, under the terms of his will, none of the Bedard children would inherit anything. My father's fortune, estimated to be in the millions of dollars, was to be left to his wife and three surviving children.

The lawyers made a point of letting me know that I would have no claims against my father's estate. I was not surprised, nor did I care.

My fight for my rightful name never had anything to do with money. It was beyond all of that. It is and always was about principle and dignity. It was and is about defending my mother.

It had never occurred to any of the DeMoulases that in the absence of DNA evidence, a judge would grant me my name. They had lost, but nevertheless, they had no intention of enabling me to secure that indisputable evidence.

Despite the fact that it is against their Greek Orthodox religion, my father's family agreed he would be cremated upon his death. No body meant no proof.

Six months later, I was on vacation in Palm Beach, Florida. It was March 8, 2000. A little after eight o'clock in the morning, the phone rang. It was my brother John, calling to tell me our father had died. I received the news with mixed emotions, but mostly I felt a deep sadness. I was sad because to his dying day, my father denied that I was his son. I suppose I shouldn't have been surprised that to the last, John refused to acknowledge my siblings and me. I guess he was always living a life in some strange state of denial that what he had done was anything out of the ordinary for a guy his age and with his own twisted perception of the world. Yet the news of John's death hit me hard. It drove home the points that I would never again have to face him and that his denial of us would forever remain as a falsehood threaded into the core of the family fabric, both his and mine.

I was sad because during all those years, I had lived with a misplaced hope. I had dared to dream that one day, my father, John DeMoulas, would tell me he regretted the way he had lived his life and was now prepared to take responsibility and make amends for the pain he had caused my mother and her family.

I was sad because it was now no longer possible for John DeMoulas to admit—if not to the world, then at least to me—that he was my father.

When my father died, it had been several years since I had last seen him. I don't think he had spoken to my mother in more than fifteen years.

There were many questions I'd wanted to ask him. Why did he keep having children with my mother? Did he ever love her? Did he ever think that driving up to the door of our housing project in his black Cadillac, knowing that there was no food to feed his children, was even close to being morally justifiable?

Was he, in fact, the untouchable eldest son in a Greek family for whom there were no consequences for behavior, no litmus test for morality, and no responsibility for taking care of a family, no matter how it was created?

Did he drink too hard and too long at his house on a New Hampshire lake in order to forget about us? Did he ever think about us? Did his wife know about my mother and his bastard children—a shadow family living in a parallel universe?

As a result of his reckless, indifferent behavior, five children were born to an unwed mother, powerless to defend herself against the DeMoulas empire. Like many children in shadow families, my brothers and sisters and I soldiered on, albeit with limited resources with which to fight our battles.

Like my father, my uncle Mike, his family, and my uncle George's family never deigned to acknowledge the relationship that had existed for so long between John DeMoulas and my mother, Dorothy Bedard—a relationship that had resulted in the birth of five illegitimate children who grew up starving in every sense of the word.

We Bedards were a disgrace to the DeMoulases. However, none of us were responsible for the fact that the distinguished, wealthy, and powerful DeMoulas family had a philanderer in its midst. John's misdeeds were swept under the rug and forgotten, but I wasn't about to let his family forget about us. We weren't garbage. We were people, and we deserved acknowledgment from those who would just as soon have forgotten we existed.

As fate once again would have it—there's no other explanation—one of my house-cleaning clients was a woman named Marianne, a judge in the Massachusetts Family Court. Over the years, she had always been sympathetic to my efforts to claim my rightful name and, in several instances, had to excuse herself from hearing my case.

Marianne lived with a nurse named Joan, who, by some odd coincidence, was one of the private-duty nurses hired to look after my father. He was being cared for at my half brother Jack's house in Andover, Massachusetts, a wealthy Boston suburb. Joan was with my father when he was pronounced dead.

Joan, of course, knew me and knew of my ongoing battle.

Joan had been given strict orders not to say anything to anyone about my father's death, where his body was being taken, or any of the details about funeral arrangements.

After she left the house in Andover, she called and told me my father was dead and what she knew about the family's plans. The family was determined to keep me from getting the DNA swab I needed to prove beyond a shadow of a doubt that John was my father. The family was going to have John cremated. They hadn't planned a grand funeral, which didn't surprise me, considering all the trouble the family was dealing with at the time. John was a real charmer, but anyone who knew him knew that the smile revealed an inherent weakness in his soul. Anyone who really knew him knew he was no good.

"This phone call never took place, George," she said. "You never heard any of this from me."

As soon as I hung up the phone, I knew I had to act quickly. I called my attorney, Ellen Poster, and we devised a plan to obtain my father's DNA. That afternoon, I was on a flight back to Boston.

I met Ellen at the Cambridge courthouse at 8:30 a.m. the next day. She asked me if I had been able to determine the location of the crematory where my father's body had been taken. I had found out that there was only one crematory in the area, and it was in Haverhill, Massachusetts. I gave her the name and phone number. Ellen called and asked to speak to the director.

We were right on the money.

Later that day, on March 9, 2000, Ellen filed a short order of notice on motion for DNA testing and a temporary restraining order enjoining the family from destroying my father's remains. The court approved both filings, and the order to obtain the DNA sample was sent via fax to the Dewhirst and Conte Funeral Home in Andover and to the Linwood Cemetery and Crematory in Haverhill.

Reportedly, there were numerous calls made from the DeMoulas family home in Lowell to the director at Linwood in an attempt to convince him to destroy my father's body. The director told the family that due to the court order, they could not destroy the body. Linwood was not willing to risk a lawsuit, not even for the DeMoulases.

So the DNA swab heard round the New England legal community was obtained and sent off to Lab Corp in North Carolina to be analyzed and compared with my mother's and mine.

When I called my mother to tell her about John, I said, "Ma, the Greek is dead." She was quiet. There was nothing left to say. It had been years since she and my father had spoken. I am certain that knowing the man she had once loved and to whom she had foolishly entrusted her life was dead brought forth a roller coaster of emotions. And in that moment, she was forced to look back to another time, when she was young, beautiful, and full of hope.

There were no calling hours for my father, and his funeral was by invitation only. Strangely, I later learned that neither Uncle Mike nor Aunt Ann, my father's sister, chose to attend.

Within a matter of a few weeks, the DNA results came back from Lab Corp, with 99.6 percent confirmation that I am the son of John DeMoulas. And now my brothers and sisters can all make the same claim if they choose. It's entirely up to them.

Shortly after my father died, I spoke with Jack DeMoulas, my father's son and my half brother. He is the eldest child in that family, and I called to let him know that my intentions were good and that I had no interest in any money from the estate.

Jack said, "Wait a minute, wait a minute—after my mother passes away, maybe we talk again but certainly not while she's alive."

Was that a door opening? Was there a possibility of some sort of reconciliation? I doubt it. Would Jack ever recognize me as his half brother? I have no reason to believe he ever will. Every member of the DeMoulas family has to understand that I am living my life as George DeMoulas and, in the process, am carrying the weight of that name with all of the good and the evil associated with it. I recall that some individuals at a party I attended thought I was rich as soon as they heard my new last name. They put me up on a pedestal—until they found out I wasn't a multimillionaire. How sad it is when money directs a person's perception of another human being, when the notion that there is a boatload of cash hanging about determines whether a person is accepted or rejected.

I have my own story to tell, and that story has nothing to do with the decade-long court battle between my uncle Mike and my uncle George's family. My story has nothing to do with the greed that ripped the family apart. My story has nothing to do with money.

My story is rooted in a belief that anything is possible in life if you want it badly enough; money does not and cannot change the truth as we know it. There are important things in life that no one can buy, and there are important things in life that cannot be denied.

Regardless of the circumstances of our birth, we all have the innate ability to overcome those circumstances and to prevail, no matter how difficult the struggle might be.

I am George Arthur DeMoulas. I have overcome those circumstances. I have prevailed.

TWELVE

After my father died and the DNA results proved I was John's son, I felt a little adrift. It was strange, but the seven years of fighting in court to get him to admit he was my father helped ground me in a sort of perpetual conflict. I had a purpose, a cause, something to fight for. Now that it was all over, I wondered what would fill the void. I began to think more and more about my long-lost sister Melveen, whom my mother had given up for adoption fifty years earlier. I felt it was time to find my oldest sister. It seemed as if a part of my life was still unresolved, and it was time to close that chapter of uncertainty.

Based on comments made to me over the years, I had believed it possible that one of the DeMoulases had adopted my sister. And when opportunities had presented themselves, I had studied my girl cousins' features to see if I could detect any resemblance to my mother.

But now I no longer had any reason to think that my sister had remained within the DeMoulas family.

I contacted a national search company. They gave me a few leads, and I focused my research on Portsmouth, New Hampshire—a city just over the border and about forty-five minutes from where I was living in Lowell.

I later discovered that at the same time I began my search, my sister embarked on her own search for her birth parents. Although no one had told her directly, she had long suspected that she had been adopted. That suspicion was born out of an innate sense that she never really belonged to the family who raised her.

After experiencing difficult times as an adult, she decided she wanted to know who she was by birth and why her biological parents had put her up for adoption. She wanted to try to put together the missing pieces, hoping that would help her find an inner peace that had eluded her.

My sister Melveen was ready to find and face the truth.

Melveen remembers being driven each Sunday to Lowell as a young girl to spend time with her parents' extended family, who were members of the Greek community. And she remembers being taken to a small grocery store from time to time and seeing a man who would sometimes come out to the car and talk to her parents. She says that as she sat in the backseat, he always looked intently at her before turning to go back into the store.

She now believes that man was our grandfather, Athas "Arthur" DeMoulas.

Through a friend, Melveen found a woman who had a small business that specialized in locating and reuniting birth parents and children who had been put up for adoption. Melveen gave the woman a copy of her birth certificate, and a relatively short time later,

Melveen learned the name of her mother—our mother, Dorothy Bedard—and where she was living.

Melveen has told me that she spent a lot of time over those years fantasizing about who her biological parents were. She grew up in an extended Greek family and was aware those families rarely give up their children; it's against their culture and their nature to do so. So she assumed she had been born under some sort of compromised circumstances.

That was all she knew, or so it seemed, until her last conversation with the woman who provided the information regarding our mother.

According to Melveen, the woman asked her, "Who do you think your father was?"

Melveen answered, "I don't know. I can only guess he must have been someone important."

Then the woman said, "Take a guess."

"John DeMoulas," my sister blurted out.

"You are right on," she replied.

To this day, Melveen has no idea what prompted her response.

For years, Melveen had shopped at the DeMoulas market on Route 1 in Hampton, New Hampshire, and at one point, her son—my nephew—had worked there as a stock boy. She might have passed our father or our uncles and aunts in the aisles or even spoken to our half brothers and sisters or cousins.

Melveen wrote my mother a letter, and soon after, we all met for the first time at my mother's apartment in Lowell.

Not surprisingly, my mother found it difficult and still finds it difficult to show Melveen any real affection. I think it's because Melveen reminds her of the mother she might have been to all of us but was not. Seeing Melveen reinforces the guilt my mother will carry with her for the rest of her life.

Melveen finds it hard to reconcile the fact that she is a DeMoulas by birth and hasn't decided if she will take the DeMoulas name; someday, she says, she might hyphenate it with her current last name. I doubt she will.

Through all the conflict and despair, I've always held my mother in high regard. Sure, I've felt angry with her. I've felt as if she let my siblings and me down when she might have found some way to keep us safe from John's cruelty and indifference. But I also feel she did the best she could under the circumstances, and I believe the odds are probably pretty good that my mother would die alone and she will have died too soon, or too young, in the prime of her life.

She will have lived with an almost complete absence of joy, forgiveness, and pride. Her life will have been one filled with long days and restless nights, and even as a much older woman, she has lived in a world of alcohol, pills, and few words.

Just before she dies, what will she remember? What will have mattered most to her? She has no gift of introspection, no inner life to draw strength from. The need to just make it through never left her, and she lives only within the markers of each day.

My mother probably has a thousand stories to tell from her life, as we all do, but for her, only one defined her.

She lived a small and simple life, barely rising beyond the expectations of her childhood. Many woman have an endless supply of dreams and hope for themselves and their children; hers began and ended with John DeMoulas.

Although he was gone from her life in fourteen years and her children and grandchildren remain, she is a polarizing and isolating figure for my brothers and sisters.

I wish I could say that it was all about her loving him too much, but in truth, I think it was because she loved herself too little.

She went on to have one more relationship with a man too kind and too generous for her, and she caused his death three years after they met—in a car accident, the result of too much drinking.

There was no manslaughter charge; the court simply concluded that this was a woman who had served her time both for the crimes of her own choosing and those committed against her. The judge let her off to stay at home with her children.

I wish my siblings and I could have known our mother before John—before she had children, when she was a girl with glistening eyes. We might have seen in her someone to look at without anger or disdain.

I often wonder about how things might have been. I know it's foolish to do that, but we are all fools in our own way. I contemplate what could have been and what should have been, just as we all do. What if she and Sophie had just kept walking by the bar that night, ignoring the tap on the window and the scent of love? Would she have met a quiet man with a good job and lived modestly with a couple of kids? Would nothing more have been asked of her?

Knowing and loving John changed little. She lived in public housing for the rest of her life, until May of 2008, when she fell and broke her hip. Her health quickly and progressively worsened, and two weeks later, my mother died in the hospital on June 13, 2008. She was seventy-five years old.

Her children don't have houses in the upscale towns of Concord or Andover, but in the working-class city of Lowell. We are day laborers. I have a successful interior-design business that I started in 1997, and I own a modest condo in the Christian Hill section of Lowell. My brother John has a construction company and lives in downtown Lowell with his wife. My brother Mike works in construction and owns the condo next door to mine.

My sister Melveen still resides in Portsmouth, New Hampshire, and works for the public school system. My sister Dorothy has a prominent position at an integrated missiles facility and owns a house in the neighboring town of Dracut. My sister Patricia works in pharmaceuticals and also owns a townhouse in Dracut.

To this day, the DeMoulases keep us at arm's length, and they have made promises that never seem to prevail on any level. Their company Market Basket continues to be one of the most successful grocery stores in New England, with an annual gross in the billions of dollars.

We didn't ask our mother the painful questions; we don't want to try to understand. We react to the hurt and the losses, real and imagined.

Whom do we blame? This was a woman whose best day was a trip with John to New York City, to the Empire State Building, in the 1960s. As with the ace fighter pilot in war or the athlete who makes the play of the game, everything that came after that one day—that one moment in time—fell off the memory chart. The longing for the man overtook everything. Her dreams couldn't rest only with someone else, and because they did, the anger spilled out and tainted everything.

I have come to accept that women like my mother have a unique loneliness, one so profound and deep that it is irresolvable. In my mother's time, her life of quiet desperation, instead of fueling a revolution for a better day for women, grinded her down and made her invisible.

What did we miss? We missed some things that came with money, such as braces for our teeth or new bikes on our birthdays, but what was really heartbreaking—and it did break all of our collective hearts—was the loss of intimacy a family gives to one another. We missed being read to at night, setting the table for dinner, talking about our day at school, or having friends over.

The biggest tragedy is that she didn't even know she missed it.

What would I have wished for her? To be able to love.

Since that tap on the window, she learned that love more than hurts—it can be punishing. She sat in her apartment, where we decorated the walls with pictures of her family; she stayed there until her last days.

I think she must have always been desperate. I know that love is taught, and it is the reflection of what you see in your parents' eyes.

She did not see it in her parents' eyes, and we did not see it in hers.

EPILOGUE

I don't know how else to say it—I feel more complete as George DeMoulas than I ever did as George Bedard. My name now reflects the truth of my father's responsibility for my life. He was there at the moment of my conception, and his name is rightfully mine.

My therapist once told me I had a "big job to do." That job, as she put it, was to make a commitment to break the cycle of abuse and neglect into which I was born. I have done that, and yes, it has taken enormous effort over many years.

I am not well educated in any formal sense of the word. Two difficult years in an indifferent high school is all I can claim in regard to education. However, I have experienced a great deal in my life, and I know how things should be.

I know how great wealth looks up close, and I know what it's like to live with nothing and to expect nothing. I also know what it feels like to be unwanted, and I realize that being unwanted results in universal pain.

In many ways, I'm a lot like the Greek side of my family; I'm a lot like my uncle Mike.

I am proud, determined, and fearless, and ironically, it is those qualities within me that made possible the arduous path I followed in order to change my name.

My brothers and sisters and I all have been victimized by the patterns we experienced growing up. We have had all the problems and misery associated with addictions to drugs and alcohol. Several of my nieces and nephews were born out of wedlock and have little or no relationship with their fathers, my brothers John and Mike. My mother always had a difficult time expressing her feelings with her children and grandchildren. For her, love never came easily.

In the end, I grew tired of hearing my brothers and sisters complain that our mother was stupid, made careless decisions, and did not know how to make her life or our lives any better. Those accusations don't begin to tell the whole story. I defend my mother for who she was.

Some people have said to me that we should view our parents as people who gave us life and expect nothing more from them. That might be one way to absolve parents who fail to live up to our expectations, but the rationale doesn't change the pain.

I was also tired of people who didn't believe I was a DeMoulas. I have the same amount of DeMoulas blood in me as my half siblings and cousins. Marriage or the absence of marriage between your parents has nothing to do with your DNA.

I've chosen to tell this personal story to end that pain. I've chosen to tell this story for my mother and for my brothers and sisters.

It takes courage to truly look at yourself and to call it the way it is. When I was in therapy, I came to understand boundaries and choices. I had to do the emotional work as an adult that I never grew through as a child. Survival makes you focus on only one thing.

You have to get to a point where you can love yourself and be happy with who you are, and when you do, you will stop hurting other people. As long as you live with a lot of pain, you will find ways to make others suffer with you.

My DeMoulas half brothers, half sisters, and cousins have been torn apart by what we refer to in my Bedard family as a "Greek tragedy."

The simple dreams of my grandfather to provide a good life for his family somehow got perverted along the way. The successes he had through hard work created enormous opportunities for his children, but the wealth that resulted became a breeding ground for hubris and greed.

Today, my father, John DeMoulas, would not have gotten away with what he did. The courts and social-service agencies would have been more supportive of my mother, and the secrets of his bastard family would have been leaked out to a prying press.

I think the world is filled not with big truths about growing up but with important little truths that meld together to form the memories of our childhood. Sometimes we remember more of the bad than the good, but every child born should know that, as Bill Gates has said, "Every life is of equal value."

In the end, I am no different from anyone else. I work hard, I crack a few jokes along the way, and I don't want to wallow in what was. I have hopes and dreams, as everyone does. But I have a lot more pride than to step into any DeMoulas Market Basket store and give them my hard-earned money to buy groceries. They let me starve, and for that, I do not forgive them.

I am absolutely sure that if I can survive and find peace in my life, anyone can.

My life was not all bad. It is far from bad today. My brothers and sisters still live with a lot of anger; I try to let it go. What good does it do? Nothing can change yesterday, except how we remember it.

I am George Arthur DeMoulas, son of John DeMoulas and half brother of Jack DeMoulas, Arthur DeMoulas, Pamela DeMoulas, and the late Kathleen DeMoulas.

I am the nephew of Telemachus "Mike" DeMoulas, George DeMoulas, and Ann DeMoulas and the cousin of Arthur S. DeMoulas, Arthur T. DeMoulas, Francis DeMoulas, Gloriann DeMoulas, Fotene DeMoulas, Diane DeMoulas, and the late Evan DeMoulas.

I, JOHN A. DeMOULAS, of Gilford, County of Belknap, State of New Hampshire, hereby revoke all Wills and Codicils heretofore made by me and declare this to be my LAST WILL AND TESTAMENT.

ARTICLE I

I may leave a Memorandum stating my wishes with respect to the disposition of certain articles of my tangible personal property. Such Memorandum, however, will be simply an expression of my wishes and shall not create any trust or obligation, nor shall it be offered for probate as a part of this Will.

All tangible personal property, excluding cash and money, owned by me at my death and all policies of insurance on such tangible personal property, I give absolutely to my wife, MARION DeMOULAS, if she survives me for ninety (90) days, and if she does not so survive me, then to my issue who survive me, such issue to take per stirpes. The division among my surviving issue under this Article I shall be made by alternate choice; the first choice to be determined by lot under the direction of my Executor.

Property distributable to a minor under this Article I may be distributed by my Executor to such a minor personally, or to such minor's legal guardian, or to some other person selected by my Executor to receive such property for such minor, and the receipt of such minor, or such minor's legal guardian, or such other person, shall be a complete discharge of my Executor in regard to such distribution.

ARTICLE II

I intentionally omit any further provisions for any children or other issue of mine, presently living or hereafter born, as they have been otherwise provided for in the Trust hereinafter mentioned.

ARTICLE III

All the rest, residue and remainder of my property, real, personal and wherever situated, including any property over which I may have any power of appointment or

Will died immediately before me. Each benefit conferred herein is made on the condition precedent that the beneficiary shall accept and agree to all of the provisions of this Will and the provisions of this Article are an essential part of each and every benefit.

ARTICLE VI

The Trust Agreement executed by me on October 3, 1994, as amended, authorizes my Trustee in the exercise of its uncontrolled discretion to pay my funeral expenses, my debts, expenses of administration of my estate, all federal and state taxes in the nature of income, estate, inheritance, succession, transfer, gift or the like taxes arising or owing on my death.

All estate taxes, federal and state, and all legacy, succession, inheritance and like taxes, imposed by reason of my death which are not paid by the Trustee referred to above, and any interest thereon, shall be paid out of the general assets of my estate as an expense of administration. So far as practicable and reasonable, my Executor may settle and compromise and shall pay as soon as convenient after my death any of the taxes referred to in the preceding sentence on future or contingent interests. Any generation-skipping tax resulting from a transfer occurring under this Will shall be charged to the property constituting the transfer in the manner provided by applicable law.

My funeral expenses, my debts and the expenses of administration of my estate, to the extent that they are not paid by my Trustee referred to above, shall be paid out of the general assets of my estate as an expense of administration.

ARTICLE VII

I give my Executor the following powers and discretions:

A. If my Executor in good faith decides that there is uncertainty as to the inclusion of particular property in my gross estate for federal estate tax purposes, he shall exclude such property from my gross estate in the estate tax return. My Executor shall not be liable for any loss to my estate or to any beneficiary, if such loss results from its decision made in good faith that there is uncertainty as to the inclusion of particular property in my gross estate.

disposal, I give, devise and bequeath to the Trustees serving at the time of the distribution of my estate under the "JOHN A. DeMOULAS LIVING REVOCABLE TRUST" dated October 3, 1994, and executed by me as Settlor and by JOHN A. DeMOULAS as Trustee, as amended by "FIRST AMENDMENT TO THE JOHN A. DeMOULAS LIVING REVOCABLE TRUST" dated __1/14__, 19 99. The said property shall be added to and become a part of the property held by the Trustees serving under said Trust Agreement to be held subject to the original terms and provisions as modified by any amendment or amendments made by me and in effect at my death whether made before or after the execution of this Will, or of any Codicil hereto.

ARTICLE IV

Insofar as I have failed to provide in this Will for any of my issue, whether born before or after my death, such failure is intentional and not occasioned by accident or mistake.

ARTICLE V

If any beneficiary hereunder shall contest the probate or validity of this Will or any provision hereof, or shall institute or join in (except as a party defendant) any proceeding to contest the validity of this Will or to prevent any provision hereof from being carried out in accordance with its terms (regardless of whether or not such proceedings are instituted in good faith and with probable cause), then all benefits provided for such beneficiary are revoked and such benefits shall pass to the residuary beneficiaries of this Will (other than such beneficiary) in the proportion that the share of each such residuary beneficiary bears to the aggregate of the effective shares of the residuary. If all of the residuary beneficiaries join in such contest or proceedings, then such benefit shall pass to those persons (other than the persons joining in such contest) who are living at my death and who would have been my distributee had I died intestate a resident of the State of New Hampshire, and had the person or persons contesting my

2. To respond (or take any other action necessary to prevent, abate or "clean up") as it shall deem necessary, prior to or after the initiation of enforcement action by any governmental body, to any actual or threatened violation of any environmental law affecting any of such property, the cost of which shall be payable from estate assets;

3. To settle or compromise at any time any claim against my estate or trust related to any such matter asserted by any governmental body or private party;

4. To disclaim any power which my Executor determines may cause it to incur personal liability as a result of any such matter, whether such power is set forth in my will, incorporated by reference herein, or granted or implied by any statute or rule of law; and

5. To decline to serve as Executor hereunder or, having undertaken to serve, resign at any time my Executor reasonably believes there is or may be a conflict of interest between it in its fiduciary and individual capacities by virtue of potential claims or liabilities which are or might be asserted against my estate because of the type or condition of estate assets.

K. When used in this instrument, the term "hazardous substance(s)" shall mean any substance defined as hazardous or toxic or otherwise regulated by any federal, state or local law(s), rule(s) or regulation(s) relating to the protection of the environment or human health ("environmental law(s)");

L. No Executor shall be personally liable to any beneficiary or other party interested in my estate or to any third parties, for any claim against my estate for the diminution in value of estate property resulting from matters involving hazardous substances, including any reporting of or response to (1) the contamination of estate property by hazardous substances, or (2) violations of any environmental laws related to my estate; provided that my Executor shall not be excused from liability for its own negligence or wrongful or willful acts;

M. To the maximum extent permitted by law, my Executor may withhold a distribution to a beneficiary hereunder until receiving from the beneficiary an indemnification agreement in which the beneficiary agrees to indemnify the Executor against any claims filed against the Executor as an "owner" or "operator" under the Comprehensive Environmental Response, Compensation, and Liability Act of 1980, as from time to time amended, or any regulation thereunder, or any other environmental law; provided further that my Executor may not take any action under this paragraph which would in any way jeopardize any marital deduction available under federal or state law for property passing to or for the benefit of my spouse; and

E. To improve or develop real estate; to construct, alter or repair buildings or structures on real estate; to settle boundary lines or easements and other rights with respect to real estate; to partition and to join with co-owners and others in dealing with real estate in any way;

F. To employ investment counsel, custodians of estate property, brokers, agents and attorneys;

G. To pay as income the whole of the interest, dividends, rent or similar receipts from property whether wasting or not and although bought or taken at a value above par, but if it is deemed advisable when property is bought or taken at a value above par, a portion of the income may be retained to offset such a loss to the principal; to treat as income or principal or to apportion between them stock dividends, extra dividends, rights to stock or securities, and proceeds from the sale of real estate, although such real estate may have been wholly or partly unproductive; to charge to income or principal or to apportion between them investment counsel's compensation, custodian's compensation, broker's commissions, agents' compensations, attorneys' fees, insurance premiums, repairs or improvements, taxes (income, estate, inheritance or any other taxes), depreciation charges, executor's compensation; and generally to determine all questions as between income and principal or to apportion between them any receipt or gain and any charge, disbursement or loss as is deemed advisable in the circumstances of each case as it arises, notwithstanding any statute or rule of law for distinguishing income from principal or any determination of the courts;

H. When paying legacies or dividing or distributing my estate, to make such payments, divisions or distribution wholly or partly in kind by allotting and transferring specific securities or other personal or real property or undivided interests therein as a part or whole of any one or more payments or shares at current values;

I. To keep any or all of the estate property at any place or places in the State of New Hampshire or elsewhere within the United States or abroad or with a depository or custodian at such place or places;

J. I also give my Executor power, exercisable in the discretion of my Executor, to deal with matters involving the actual or threatened contamination of property held in my estate (including any interests in sole proprietorships, partnerships or corporations and any assets owned by such business enterprises) by hazardous substances, or involving compliance with environmental laws. In particular, my Executor is empowered:

   1. To inspect and monitor any such property periodically, as it deems necessary, to determine compliance with any environmental law affecting such property, with all expenses of such inspection and monitoring to be paid from the income or principal of the estate;

business interest, and it is to be exempt from any liability for any loss whatsoever for its acts done in or decisions made in good faith relative thereto. My Executor is authorized to loan to or borrow money for such business, or to or for any corporation in such manner as it may deem advisable, including the power to select or vote for the appointment or election of persons and managers, officers or directors who may also be partners or employees of my Executor or my Executor himself.

ARTICLE X

In extension and not in limitation of the powers given by law or other provisions of this Will, my Executor shall have the following powers with respect to the settlement of my estate, in each case, to be exercised from time to time in the discretion of my Executor and without notice or order or license of court:

A. To retain any investments, and during the period of administration of my estate, to invest and reinvest in stocks, shares and obligations of corporations, of unincorporated associations or trusts and of investment companies or in a common trust fund, or in any other kind of personal or real property, notwithstanding the fact that any or all of the investments made or retained are of a character or size which but for this express authority would not be considered proper for Executors;

B. To sell, at public or private sale, to exchange, to lease and to make contracts concerning real or personal property for such considerations and upon such terms as to credit or otherwise as my Executor may determine, which leases and contracts may extend beyond the term of settlement of my estate; to give options therefor; to execute deeds, transfers, leases, and other instruments of any kind; to sell estate property on the installment basis;

C. To hold bonds, shares or other securities in bearer form, or in the name of my Executor or in the name of a nominee, without indication of any fiduciary capacity; to deposit cash in a checking or savings account in a bank, without indication of a fiduciary capacity;

D. To give general or special proxies or powers of attorney for voting or acting in respect of shares or securities, which may be discretionary and with power of substitution; to deposit shares or securities with, or transfer them to, protective committees or similar bodies; to join in any reorganization and to pay assessments or subscriptions called for in connection with shares or securities held by my Executor;

B. The decision of my Executor as to the date which should be selected for the valuation of property in the gross estate for federal estate tax purposes shall be conclusive on all concerned.

C. When a choice is available as to whether certain deductions shall be taken as income tax deductions or estate tax deductions, the decision of my Executor in this regard shall be conclusive on all concerned and no adjustment of income and principal accounts in the estate need be made as a result of such decision.

D. To join with my said wife or her Executor or Administrator, in filing a joint federal or state income tax return of the income of my said wife and myself for any period or periods for which such a return may be permitted.

E. To agree with my said wife or her Executor or Administrator as to how the burden of the liability for federal or state income tax, or interest thereon, arising out of the filing of a joint return by my Executor and my said wife or her Executor or Administrator, shall be borne as between my estate and my said wife or her estate.

F. To consent for federal gift tax purposes to gifts made by my said wife as having been made one-half (1/2) by me and one-half (1/2) by her.

ARTICLE VIII

My Executor is authorized to make partial or complete distribution to estate beneficiaries from time to time during administration; to distribute unequal amounts to similar beneficiaries from time to time during administration, and to make such other distributions during administration as it may determine.

ARTICLE IX

If I have during my lifetime made arrangements for the sale or other disposition of any business interest, corporate or otherwise, that I may have at my death, then I direct my Executor to carry out such agreement or agreements as expeditiously as possible, and I expressly leave to the discretion of my Executor the retention, continuancy, sale, liquidation or other disposition of any other such business interest I may have at my death, knowing that he will take into consideration with respect thereto the wishes and best interests of my family, and he is specifically empowered to take all steps which he deems necessary or advisable in connection with any such business or

N. To do all other acts in its judgment necessary or desirable for the proper and advantageous management, investment, and distribution of my estate.

ARTICLE XI

I nominate and appoint my wife, MARION DeMOULAS, of Gilford, New Hampshire, to be Executrix of this Will. If my said Executrix shall be unable to act as Executrix because of death, resignation or any other reason, then my son, DOUGLAS J. DeMOULAS, of Andover, Massachusetts, shall be Successor Executor under this Will. Any Successor Executor under this Will shall succeed to all the power, including discretionary powers, herein granted to my Executrix. I request that the same person or persons named herein as Executor, upon application, be appointed Temporary Executor without any notice, in the same order of succession. I request that any Executor or Temporary Executor appointed under this Will be exempt from furnishing any sureties on his or her official bond.

ARTICLE XII

All references to my Executors hereunder shall be deemed to include all successors to my Executors. My Executors shall be liable only for their own acts or omissions in bad faith. No one dealing with my Executors need inquire concerning the validity of anything that they purport to do or need see to the application of any money paid or any property transferred to or upon the order of my Executors. My Executors shall not be liable for the acts, omissions or defaults of any agent appointed with due care.

ARTICLE XIII

Throughout this Will the masculine gender shall be deemed to include the feminine and the neuter, the singular to denote the plural, and vice-versa, where the context so requires.

ARTICLE XIV

I request that the representation of persons unborn or unascertained be dispensed with in the allowance of any accounting presented to the court by my Executors.

ARTICLE XV

In the event that my said wife and I shall be killed in a common accident or as a result of a common disaster, or under such circumstances that there is no sufficient evidence that we died other than simultaneously, it shall be presumed that my wife survived me and this presumption shall apply throughout this Will, but if any other person entrusted hereunder and I should die under circumstances which render it doubtful as to which of us died first it shall be presumed that I survived such person.

IN WITNESS WHEREOF, I hereunto set my hand and seal this _____ day of ____1/14____, 19_99_. For identification, I have signed each of the foregoing pages of this Will.

_____
JOHN A. DeMOULAS

On this __14__ day of __January__, 19__99__, JOHN A. DeMOULAS, the above named testator signed, published and declared the foregoing instrument, to be his Last Will and Testament, in the presence of us, who, thereupon, at his request and in his presence, and in the presence of each other, subscribed our names hereto as witnesses.

_____
NAME

9 Parkridge Hill Rd
Andover MA 01810
ADDRESS

_____
NAME

1601 Corporate Drive
Boynton Bch, FL 33426
ADDRESS

STATE OF Florida
COUNTY OF Palm Beach   DATED: 1/14 , 19 99

We, JOHN A. DeMOULAS, Douglas J. DeMoulas , and Linette S. Potter , the testator and witnesses, respectively, whose names are signed to the attached or foregoing instrument, being first duly sworn, do hereby declare to the undersigned authority that the testator signed and executed the instrument as his Last Will and that he has signed willingly or directed another to sign for him, and that he executed it as his free and voluntary act for the purposes therein expressed; and that each of the witnesses, at the request of the testator, in his presence, and in the presence of each other, signed the Will as witness and that to the best of his or her knowledge, the testator was at that time eighteen (18) or more years of age, of sound mind and under no constraint or undue influence.

_____
TESTATOR

_____
WITNESS

_____
WITNESS

Subscribed, sworn to and acknowledged before me by JOHN A. DeMOULAS, the Testator and subscribed and sworn to before me by Douglas J DeMoulas , and Linette S. Potter , the witnesses, on the date first above-written.

_____
Notary Public
My Commission Expires: Sept 10, 2001

OFFICIAL NOTARY SEAL
STEPHEN E CHAMBERS
NOTARY PUBLIC STATE OF FLORIDA
COMMISSION NO. CC697916
MY COMMISSION EXP. SEPT 10,2001

www.ingramcontent.com/pod-product-compliance
Lightning Source LLC
LaVergne TN
LVHW041622070526
838199LV00052B/3213